The Path of Least Resistance
for Managers

Other books by Robert Fritz:

The Path of Least Resistance

Creating

Corporate Tides

THE PATH
of LEAST
RESISTANCE
for MANAGERS

Designing Organizations to Succeed

ROBERT FRITZ

Foreword by Peter Senge

Berrett-Koehler Publishers
San Francisco

Berrett-Koehler Publishers, Inc.
450 Sansome Street, Suite 1200
San Francisco, CA 94111-3320
Tel: 415-288-0260   Fax: 415-362-2512
Website: www.bkpub.com

Ordering Information

Individual sales. Berrett-Koehler publications are available through most bookstores. They can also be ordered direct from Berrett-Koehler at the address above.

Quantity sales. Special discounts are available on quantity purchases by corporations, associations, and others. For details, contact the "Special Sales Department" at the Berrett-Koehler address above.

Orders for college textbook/course adoption use. Please contact Berrett-Koehler Publishers at the address above.

Orders by U.S. trade bookstores and wholesalers. Please contact Publishers Group West, 1700 Fourth Street, Berkeley, CA 94710; 510-528-1444; 1-800-788-3123; fax 510-528-9555.

Printed in the United States of America

 Printed on acid-free and recycled paper that is composed of 85 percent recycled waste, including 10 percent postconsumer waste.

Library of Congress Cataloging-in-Publication Data
Fritz, Robert. 1943–
    The path of least resistance for managers : designing
organizations to succeed / Robert Fritz : foreword by Peter Senge.
        p.   cm.
    Includes bibliographical references and index.
    ISBN 1-57675-065-5
    1. Management.   2. Organization.   I. Title
HD31.F758   1999
658—dc21   99-12000
                                         CIP

First Edition

02 01 00 99   10 9 8 7 6 5 4 3 2 1

Designed by Detta Penna

I am a fortunate man, especially in one regard, and
that is my wife, to whom I dedicate this book.

She is a true friend, professional colleague, partner
in life, and total inspiration. We are a team, and
even though I have written this book, her spirit,
support, and wisdom have had great impact on me.

So, to you, Rosalind, you wonder, you love, you
penetrating mind, you poetic heart . . .
to you.

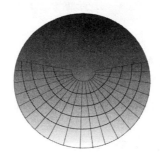

Contents

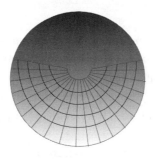

Foreword

Peter Senge

"Results-based management" has a bad name these days. It is typical to hear people lament that "all that matters around here is the bottom line." Bosses everywhere focus people "on the numbers" and seek to motivate them to perform. Yet few organizations perform up to their potential, and, ironically, the inability to realize that potential is a deep source of dissatisfaction among most organizations' members. No one wants to be on a mediocre team.

Herein lies a deep puzzle. Results truly matter to people. Yet focusing on the results is often a poor way to succeed—at least the way it is typically done in most organizations.

This situation reminds me of those old movies we've all seen of people trying to fly in machines before the airplane was invented: machines that had flapping wings; machines that had big, circular, umbrella-like contraptions that moved up and down; machines that had four sets of wings, none of which was large enough to generate sufficient lift. Despite their differences, all these inventions achieved the same result: they were incapable of sustained flight. It didn't matter how hard the pilots tried. It didn't matter how imaginative or clever they were. It didn't matter how good they were as people or how noble their aspirations were. There was nothing these pilots were going to do to make these inventions fly—because they were structurally incapable of flight.

This is precisely why most organizations fail to fly as well. The structures that their members create are incapable of generating the results they truly desire. It doesn't matter how hard people try, how good they are as people, or how lofty their aspirations are. There is nothing people are going to do to create the results of which they are potentially capable given the structures that predominate. And, worst of all, very few people are even aware of the problem. Almost everyone is busy trying to get the wings to flap faster, rather than asking the questions that might begin to reveal the structural causes of their limitation.

As an accomplished musician, composer, painter, and filmmaker, Robert Fritz brings a unique perspective to this puzzle: the perspective of the creative process. Fritz regards the creative process—understanding how people bring into reality what they seek to create—as "the greatest invention in human history." The creative process underlies all creative arts, as well as much of sciences, especially when scientific understanding is aimed at invention. For the last twenty-five years, Robert has been helping people in organizations understand the principles of the creative process. "Initially, I was interested in just helping people get better at creating," he says. "But gradually, I became more and more fascinated by organizations themselves and how they operated structurally."

Fritz argues that there are two dominant structural dynamics that shape how organizations function. Organizations that consistently "advance" do so because "structural tension" dominates. Those who consistently "oscillate" do so because "structural conflict" dominates. The entirety of this book is devoted to explaining how these two dynamics operate—why in some organizations "success leads to success" while other organizations consistently struggle—and how the members of an organization can influence which dynamic shapes their destiny.

Structural conflict predominates when people find that they are trapped, repeatedly, between the proverbial "rock and a hard place." Organizations want innovation, but innovation requires risks and failure, and organizations also want to avoid failure. Organizations want loyal customers, but being committed to your customers may mean seeing things that you are doing that do not add value to customers, and people don't want to lose their jobs. Organizations encourage people to speak out about what they see as problems limiting success, but speaking out may mean saying things that are threatening to others and that can get you in trouble.

The theory of structural conflict explains how people consistently, and often sincerely, espouse the importance of being results-oriented and yet produce organizations that work in the opposite fashion. In essence, many other considerations supersede the espoused pursuit of results—like maintaining power, not upsetting the boss, looking good, and avoiding surprises. Recently a retired CEO, famous in Europe and the United States for his business accomplishments, commented in private, "I have never been around a corporation where at least two-thirds of management's attention wasn't devoted to making one another feel OK."

On the other hand, structural tension characterizes those organizations that know what it means, practically, to honor vision and reality in equal measure. Such organizations do not shy away from facing difficult situations. Indeed, for them reality is an ally—telling the truth anchors them in the here-and-now without weighing them down. Such organizations operate predominantly in the creative orientation (versus the reactive organization) because they see whatever happens as creating the conditions from which they must currently move in pursuit of their aspirations. In organizations in which structural tension dominates, structural conflicts still exist, but they too are seen as one more aspect of current reality, one more feature about which people must acknowledge the present in the service of creating the future.

Fritz's perspective on the creative process differs markedly from much of what is written today on "more creative" approaches to management. For example, there is a great deal of interest today in "self-organization"—how, if managers would stop trying to organize and control everything, systems would self-organize. This is an understandable reaction to the tendency of traditional management to overcontrol. But it often leaves the impression that managers should just leave people alone, that people will automatically organize effectively. The problem is that activities in organizations often self-organize into structural conflicts, not structural tension. And once these structural conflicts become embedded, they shape how the organization functions. The dilemmas become undiscussable, and, after a while, the structural conflicts become taken for granted, so much so that people do not even see them anymore. They are "just how things are."

What is often missing in the quest for management beyond rigid hierarchical control is what has been understood in the creative arts for a very long time. There is no substitute for discipline and self-control. Many have artistic talent but never develop that talent because they lack the required discipline. Discipline is not "natural" in the sense that it occurs without effort. Discipline is focused effort, guided by principles and practical tools. The discipline that is lacking in most organizations is evident by the fact that everyone is busy fixing problems, and few are seeking to understand what is really going on. We would rather just fix things now and then deal with the next problems once we "get there." Often, it doesn't even seem that there is an alternative. If anything, reactiveness in organizations has grown as a way of life in recent years with financial stress, downsizing, and increased workloads. This reactiveness just increases the tendency for structural conflicts to dominate—because no one has the time for the reflection and serious conversation to make it otherwise.

Likewise, Fritz's perspective on structure is quite different from almost everything that has been written on the subject in the social sciences over the past fifty years. Again, I think these distinctions come from his background in the creative arts. Unlike most social scientists who analyze social structures, Fritz focuses primarily on creating structures that can move organizations in the directions their members seek. In this way, his orientation, in my judgment, is more like that of most organization members, whose ultimate interest is in planes that fly rather than in analysis of why no flight is occurring.

I first began working with Robert Fritz over twenty years ago. He has been a friend and mentor ever since, never ceasing to amaze me with his ability to penetrate complex subjects and articulate simple principles that guide effective action. But this simplicity can be misunderstood. The difference between simplicity that trivializes and simplicity that illuminates defines genius. In this day and age of quick-fix nostrums and management books that excel at making trivial ideas complicated, it is rare to find simplicity based on deep understanding, verified from extensive first-hand experience.

I sincerely hope that this new book brings the attention and serious study Fritz's work deserves. He is an extraordinary inventor, whose work is distinctively nonderivative. For those of us used to books about management and organizations that seem to have been written from 50,000 feet above, his work is very much "on the ground," with examples from "the inside out"—real people and real organizations learning to create real results that matter to them.

The Path of Least Resistance for Managers is not the last word on structure. It is probably more like the first word. But, for many people concerned with building organizations that are more capable and more exciting, it is a great starting point.

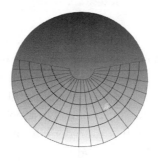

Acknowledgments

There are many people who have contributed their talents, insights, wisdom, and energy to this book. And I am grateful to them all. I am grateful to you, Jacques de Spoelberch, friend and literary agent, for your untiring work as champion of *The Path of Least Resistance for Managers*, in particular, and my literary endeavors, in general. Over the years, and through many book projects, you have always been a tremendous support, colleague, and mentor.

I am grateful to you, Steven Piersanti, publisher of Berrett-Koehler, for your support of this project. You guided me, coached me, and inspired me. Thank you. And thank you Charles Dorris, who served as the major editor for this project. Your insight was superb, your skill masterful, and your impact great. And thank you, Elizabeth Swenson, production director, for overseeing the process of turning the manuscript into a book. And thank you, Detta Penna, for your special gift of book design, and the special way you applied your gift on behalf of this book. And thank you, Barbara Kimmel, for the way your copyediting helped turn my most clumsy sentences into lovely phrases that expressed just what I was trying to say. And thank you, Katherine Lee, for proofreading the book cover to cover. And speaking of covers, thank you, Cassandra Chu, for your brilliant cover design.

And many thanks to Berrett-Koehler's marketing team, a group of crackerjack professionals who know how to bring a book to market in ways that are truly consistent with the book itself. This is rare in your industry, and as an author, I am grateful.

I am also grateful to you, Frank Newton and Melissa Astley, of the Robert Fritz, Inc. staff. Your dedication and untiring work on behalf of this book has been the glue that has held much of the project together.

I am grateful to the many structural consultants with whom I work. You are forging a new frontier that helps us all discover a new land. I am grateful to the many companies that have been the among the first to employ the structural approach in their organizations over the years. You have proven the power and good business sense of structural thinking.

And thank you, Peter Senge, for your kind foreword to this book, and for the many years of friendship and inspiration, moments of fun and profundity. You are truly one of the great people on the planet, and I am privileged to know you.

And I am grateful to you, my wife Rosalind, beyond anything I could ever say in words, even though I love trying to say it to you. I don't think it's a secret to any who know us how much I love and adore you.

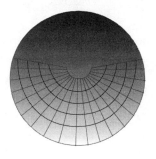

Prologue

Crossing the frontier of the old West, settlers in covered wagons found that much of their route was already laid out for them to follow. It had been forged by herds of the Great Plains bison as they moved across the terrain through the previous centuries.

Later, when track was laid for railroads, surveyors found their best routes were these very same buffalo paths that pointed the way to the Rockies and beyond to the Promised Land of California. The master railroad designers of the nineteenth century chose these trails because they were the best ones anyone could have developed. The buffalo had found the optimal passage and anticipated the future movement across the vast continent.

How did these magnificent animals accomplish such a feat? They followed the principle of *the path of least resistance*. As they moved through the land, they placed one foot in front of the next. Each step guided the next step. What determined each step was the topography—the contour of the earth. When faced with a sudden incline, a group of rocks, or a thorny stubble, the bison would adjust their course and seek the easiest next step.

Step led to step and way led to way, deepening the path over time. Each new herd that traveled through the land found it natural to move where their predecessors had gone before.

The bison were following the laws of nature. We all do, as we all must, whether we like it or not. And in nature, *energy moves where it is easiest to go*. This is the principle of the path of least resistance.

Water in a riverbed must follow the path of least resistance, as must electrons through a circuit, as must wind blowing through a canyon, as must weather patterns crossing the planet. As we do, ourselves, as we pass through our lives.

The phrase "the path of least resistance" has two distinct meanings: one colloquial, and one scientific. The colloquial meaning is *the easy way out*. "Al took the path of least resistance" may mean that Al was a lazy, slipshod creep who avoided the necessary hard work and, consequently, produced a lousy outcome. This is not the meaning of the phrase in this book.

We will use the scientific insight, which is that *energy moves along the path of least resistance*. In other words, energy moves where it is easiest to go.

This is as true for organizations within the multinational corporate world as it is for water flowing through a riverbed and blood surging through the bloodstream.

We all understand this principle, but we forget it when we think about our organizations or about our own lives. And yet, the principle is always in operation. It never sleeps. It never goes on vacation. It never takes a day off. We may seem to move from situation to situation or event to event or financial quarter to financial quarter or year to year. But through it all, we are moving along the path of least resistance.

Sometimes the path leads us to great difficulty, sometimes to easy success. Sometimes the path will lead us to be able to accomplish great deeds, and other times lead us to banging our heads against the wall.

The path changes and as it changes, we must go along. So, when we're in the thick of it and all hell is breaking loose, and we feel that we've done our best, but that our best wasn't good enough, and that other people were the ones who really screwed up and we are paying the price . . . we are in that situation because the path of least resistance has brought us there.

I know that this can be a terribly uncomfortable thought at first glance. But it also can be a comforting thought as well, because if in nature we can travel only the path of least resistance (scientific meaning), then for us to go somewhere else, we need to form a *different* path of least resistance. And that's what this book is all about.

The things we have tried in the past that haven't worked can lead us to a conclusion—that our path of least resistance didn't support the cause and must have led us in a different direction than we wanted to go. This observation can be made about your organizational work and about your life. The path *unchanged* equals more of the same patterns. The path *changed* equals new possibilities for success.

The primary strategy of this book is to take the principle of the path of least resistance seriously. Once we do, we can recognize that when we are having difficulties and things are getting tougher, anything we do to change the situation won't work in the long term if we haven't rerouted the path of least resistance. We will see why the great majority of organizational change efforts that have been tried have failed. We will see that often it's not the content of the change— be it TQM, reengineering, or the flavor of the month—but that the path of least resistance didn't support those change efforts within those organizations, even though the same approach may have worked well in other organizations.

If we truly understand the profundity of the principle of the path of least resistance, we come to realize that often we are in situations that have their own rules and laws, and that we must follow these rules and laws whether we like it or not, and whether we know about them or not. Nature is not a mother we can go against for long before she proves her dominance over our lives and organizations. You can't fool Mother Nature, *but you can be fooled by Mother Nature.*

Sometimes we may feel that we are at the short end of Robert Frost's wonderfully clever prayer poem:

> Forgive, O Lord, my little jokes on Thee
> And I'll forgive Thy great big one on me.

Organizational life can feel as if there is order on top and chaos and disorder underneath. So people go about their business, and yet there seems to be this demon in the basement that makes their best efforts go astray. We can feel a little like Frost's notion of an ironic Cosmic joke being played in which we are the simple pawns who get it in the neck for someone or something else's pleasure.

It can feel that way *when we don't know the causes in play.* From our point of view, we do our best—what more can anyone ask?—but then "poof," we're in trouble. What the heck is going on?

When we come to understand the true causes, we begin to see that there is both rhyme and reason in the events that occur. What we thought was chaos and disorder transforms itself into clarity and order. We can see how the path of least resistance has led us to places we didn't want to be. We can also understand how to change the path of least resistance so that it leads us to where we do want to be.

In this book, we're not talking theory, but practice based on principles. The principles are from nature. Why try to fool Mother Nature when you can create a strategic alliance with her? She's a good lady to have on your side.

All the people within your organization are in the same boat, which is traveling along the path of least resistance. The more people within the organization who understand the principles in this book, the better. But if even one person gets it—you, for example—there can be quite a change that can happen for the entire company.

This is a hands-on book for hands-on managers who face the real-world challenges, day in and day out. It's for senior managers who are faced with business strategy and overall direction of the company, as well as for middle managers who face the tasks of getting the company where it is trying to go. It's for project managers who create products and systems that fuel the fire, and for people who have the fiduciary responsibilities who make the money aspects of the organization work. When we have insight about the path of least resistance, we can redesign our organizations so that they work better than ever before.

Three Insights

This book is based on three insights that are the fundamental principles of the path of least resistance. By understanding and working with these principles, we can learn to master the management of our organizations and personal and professional situations.

The first insight is that energy moves along the path of least resistance.

Our organizations move along this path, as do our personal and professional lives. Any changes we attempt to make that do not take the path of least resistance into account, and inadvertently violate the path of least resistance, will not work. And this is the major reason that change effort after change effort often doesn't work over time. The changes might be excellent in and of themselves. But they can be imposed on an organization against the path of least resistance, and, consequently, they fail again and again. In those cases, the path of least resistance is to resist the change.

The second insight is just as fundamental. It is:

The underlying structure of anything will determine its path of least resistance.

The topography in the old West determined the route the bison chose. Had the topography been different, the bison would have walked along a different path. The path of least resistance does not come into being arbitrarily. Instead, it is forged by an underlying structure.

Structure determines the path of least resistance, and organizations are subject to inescapable structural laws that govern their behavior. Much of this book takes into account the laws and principles of structure so we can understand why an organization can move from this business strategy to that, from this management approach to that, from this marketing approach to that. Through our study of structure, we can understand why some organizations perform like high-performance racecars, and some perform like low-tech rocking chairs.

The third insight provides us with hope and self-determination. It is:

We can determine the path of least resistance by creating new structures.

Just as the Army Corps of Engineers can change a riverbed, and thereby change the flow of water, we can change the underlying structures of our organizations, and even of our lives. A change of structure leads to a change of the path of least resistance.

We can redesign our organizations so that the path of least resistance begins to flow in the direction we want our organizations to go. But it takes work to learn how to do this. Like many things in life, often the principles are easier to talk about than they are to implement. Redesigning the organization is at least a two-step process: *understanding* first, *application* second. The application requires us to be diligent, rigorous, thoughtful, honest, disciplined, and creative. It's not an easy path, but it is the best one for the organization and the men and women within the organization. *But without the first step— understanding—the second step is impossible.* Learn these lessons well, and you will stack the cards in your favor.

"Captain, I cannot break the laws of structure."

The designer of the high-performance racing car must take the laws of physics into account in his or her work, as must the designer of low-tech rocking chairs. As *Star Trek's* Scottie has said, "Captain, I cannot break the laws of physics!" Nor can we break the laws of structure when we shift into design mode. If we are to redesign our organizations for success, we must know the inescapable structural laws that rule them, not to overcome these laws, but to work with them.

This book introduces you to nine inescapable laws of organizational structure. Each one provides us with essential insights that we can use to understand our current situations and redesign them. Since we cannot break the laws of organizational structure, our approach is to be sensitive to the workings of structure and the power of the path of least resistance. That way you can go far beyond the points you have been able to go in the past, to the achievement of your highest aspirations.

There are a group of organizations that have used a structural approach for years in building their organization. These organizations represent models that we can look to in learning the practical lessons in this book. Most of the ones I will write about are business organizations, but we will also hear from governmental organizations, public service organizations, educational organizations, and religious organizations that are using a structural approach, all with great success. These organizations illustrate the fact that the path of least resistance can be consciously formed when we understand the structural principles involved.

The three insights—(1) energy moves along the path of least resistance, (2) an underlying structure determines the path of least resistance, and (3) we can change the underlying structure and redirect the path of least resistance—form the basis of true organizational and managerial mastery. The first two insights have to do with knowledge and background. If these were the only two principles involved, all we could do is understand why things were the ways they were, but we couldn't do much with that knowledge, except be philosophical when things go wrong. It's the third insight that enables us to redesign the organization and have the redesign lead to real and lasting success.

So this book is like a design book in which we get knowledge about structure so we can use it in our redesign work. Turning principles into something you can use is the book's aim, so we can find our own path leading to the successful achievement of our dreams.

Creating What You Want

One of the major goals of this book is to help you create the organization you want. To do that, we need to understand at least two types of things.

First, we need to know how the path of least resistance is formed by the underlying structure we are in. So, we need to know something about the principles of structure. What we will learn is the actual structural reasons for oscillation and for advancement, and why they are so different. The second thing we need to learn is how to use our new-found knowledge about structure to design or redesign our organizations so they will produce the level of accomplishment and experience we want.

What you don't need is yet another business book telling you about techniques you can't actually use in your own organization. The organization will reject these new techniques, no matter how good they are, like a body rejecting an implanted organ. You need to know how to manage a structural change so that you can reroute the path of least resistance so that it leads to accomplishment and advancement. Then the techniques and processes you adopt will work to build the organization's pattern of success.

Composing the Organization

Imagine that an organization could be constructed like a great piece of orchestral music. What would it be like? It would have primary themes and secondary themes that are expressed throughout the organization. It would have accompaniment that supported the theme. All the members of the organization would be working together, playing their part and performing their unique role so that everyone else's part is supported. Leadership would be coordinating all the activities so they fall into place. And the design—the musical score—gives everyone exactly what he or she needs to understand how it all fits together.

Can managers function in a similar way to composers, conductors, and musicians? Yes. But for this metaphor to be useful, we need it to be more actual than symbolic. When managers access the type of skills and insights that the music makers need in their profession, they can put into their organization a world-class level of performance worthy of the Boston Symphony or the New York Philharmonic.

This book has two dimensions that are inextricably tied together and give you a type of compositional technique that you can use in your organization: *structural insights* and *design tools*. The design tools include a major technique that we have been using with great success in our clients' companies for over the past fifteen years. It is called *Structural Tension Charting*. This technique is the closest thing I know to a real compositional process. Using this process, we first develop main themes, and then we create important details that support the themes. Through this process, we are able to engineer a path of least resistance that leads directly to the successful achievement of our goals.

Structural Dynamics

This book refers to the work I have developed over the past twenty years, called Structural Dynamics. It is the study of how structure works within nature, within people, within personal relationships, and within organizations. Organizations are a structural phenomenon as much as anything else, and unless we understand how and why they work as structure, we will not be able to change them in predictable ways. Our attempts to improve them will fail in the end, and we will have created a host of unintended consequences that we never wanted.

There are many people in this book who are identified as Structural Consultants, a term used to describe people who have had extensive training in the subject of structure, especially as it relates to organizations. These people are able to bring their experience and knowledge of structural issues to the attention of their client organizations. Structural Consulting is a very different method of working with an organization in that it analyzes the organization's structure *first*, and then works with those insights to help redesign the organization so that the path of least resistance can lead to true success. Because of the approach, change efforts are often very successful in enabling the organization to create the results it wants.

This current book is a next generation of its predecessor, *Corporate Tides*. Those who know that book will find this one updated, redesigned and rewritten—I hope you like the changes.

There are three parts in this book; the first is "The Path to Advancement," which focuses on key principles and techniques we can use in organizational design. The second part is "The Path of Oscillation," which helps us understand why our best efforts do not always succeed, and why success sometimes leads to new problems and reversals as a product of bad structure. The third part of the book is "Elements of Design (Moving from the Rocking Chair to a Ferrari)." This part, as it sounds, helps us change the path of least resistance from oscillating to advancing structures. Each part builds on the next, and gives us a blueprint for building the most successful organizations possible, not only in business terms, but also in human terms.

The Great Possibilities

There are great possibilities for the organization to be transformed—to begin anew—no matter what the past has been, to re-create itself. Organizations can go beyond the inevitability that the future must be an extension of the past.

The principle that we are talking about is sometimes known as *transcendence*, which is the ability to start over again and be given a second chance. Within our own lives, we can be the subject of this principle and turn over a new leaf. Organizations can benefit from the same principle, redesign their fundamental structures, and reroute the path of least resistance. And my hope is that this book can make this principle of transcendence come alive in your organization in such a way that you and your colleagues can redesign the ways you work together, think together, and create together—so you can begin anew, learning the lessons of the past, but able to turn the page to new possibilities that may have been unimagined before now.

PART I

THE PATH TO
ADVANCEMENT

CHAPTER

1

An Organization's Structure
The Path to Success or Failure

One of the biggest mysteries I confronted when I first started to work with organizations was why success didn't always succeed. You would think that it would. But I saw a disturbing pattern in many "world class" multinationals: Success didn't go anywhere.

I had seen successful product development teams broken up after the product was developed, rather than be kept together "after the war" (as a friend of mine likes to say). Processes that blew away the performance of other plants within the same company were not studied by the heads of those other plants. Colleagues consistently ignored successful methods that were definitively better, quicker, and cheaper; methods that produced higher quality, etc. Nobody wanted to know about them.

But I have had the privilege of working with companies in which success did succeed. These are the true learning organizations. New methods were studied, spread, and adopted. Being smart was rewarded; being stupid was not. Fairness was the standard operating practice, and people helped each other, rather than worked against each other. These organizations were able to advance and build new success on old success or even failure.

The successful and unsuccessful organizations both follow a path of least resistance. Their underlying structure determines the path they follow. A different structure will bring us to different possibilities, and this chapter gives you an overview of structure—what it is and how it works.

What Is Structure?

First let me tell you what structure is *not*. It's not boxes on charts showing reporting relationships. Unfortunately, that's what most managers think of when they hear the term *structure*.

But who reports to whom doesn't tell us anything about the structural dynamics that drive an organization to perform and behave as it does. But that's what we need to know: the structural dynamics we confront within our own organizations.

When we think of structure, we think of girders, bridges, walls, or monuments—objects that are static, fixed, or stationary. While these structures may seem immovable and rigid, they are far from static. They have been designed to move in response to the wind or to earthquakes. And if they work as designed, they only seem stationary. To create stability, the structure must contain innumerable dynamic relationships that produce balance, strength, and solidity.

So think about structure as moving rather than stationary, and you're closer to understanding it. Think of it as a dynamic in which change is its nature.

But structure is often hard to see. We have not been trained to think structurally, so, for the most part, the structures in our lives and organizations are invisible.

The consequences of structure, however, are readily visible in the circumstances in which we find ourselves: underfunded projects that lack full support of the organization, unclear strategies, tactics that compete against other tactics within the same organization, rewards that support opposite values from the ones on the big poster hanging on the lobby wall, the major direction of the organization changing every few years, mission and vision statements that are ignored in the daily running of the company, members of the organization focused on petty stuff while ignoring the major issues they face, and so on.

All of these behaviors are consequences of a faulty structure. If we don't know anything about structure, we have little chance of changing it.

Here's a brief definition that may be helpful:

> *Structure* is an entity (such as an organization) made up of individual elements or parts (such as people, resources, aspirations, values, market trends, levels of competence, reward systems, departmental mandates, capital, workload/capacity relationships, and so on) that impact each other by the relationships they form.

Okay, maybe that definition wasn't so helpful. But let's take a closer look at what I just said.

Structure is an entity . . . In other words, it's a whole thing. When we talk about a structure, we are talking about something that has a totality to it, a wholeness. So, when we talk about the organization as a structure, we are talking about it as something that is whole and integrated.

. . . *made up of individual elements or parts* . . . Your car is made up of parts. Ask anyone in the parts department of an auto dealership. But parts alone don't make a car. Ask any mechanic. We need to know what the parts are that make up this whole thing, but we need the next part of the definition, too.

. . . *that impact each other by the relationships they form.* A car is a whole thing, which has parts, and these parts effect each other. They are there for a reason. They function together in predictable ways. Change the way they function, and you get different performance from the car. Ask any Yugo owner.

As we said earlier, organizational structure is dynamic, and like anything dynamic, it is governed by laws.

Organizations Either Advance or Oscillate

Organizations follow inescapable structural laws. They do so because they must. They have no choice about it because they have to follow the path of least resistance.

First the bad news. No matter how good our intentions may be, our organizations must be true to the structural laws that govern them.

Period. They must follow the path of least resistance. Any changes that do not take these laws into account are likely to fail, no matter how sincere we are or how good our values.

And now the good news. The inversion of the above statement is true: Organizations that take structural laws into account when redesigning themselves are likely to succeed, because a change in the underlying structure of an organization changes the path of least resistance. Then, energy tends to move most easily toward the successful accomplishment of our goals.

Laws of Organizational Structure

The nine laws of organizational structure will be discussed throughout this book. Let's look at the first two of these laws.

An organization produces from tens of thousands to millions of actions in pursuit of its goals. Coordinated or not, these actions produce overall effects that fall into one of two very different categories: *structural advancement* or *structural oscillation*. So here is the first law of organizational structure.

The FIRST Law of Organizational Structure

Organizations either oscillate or advance.

This distinction is truly as black and white as it sounds. An organization is predominately one that advances or one that oscillates. When any type of action (TQM, organizational learning, reengineering, you name it), occurs in an organization structured to advance, it has an entirely different effect than it would in an organization structured to oscillate. In the first, actions actually work; in the second, they don't.

In both types of organizations there are instances of success. In fact, every organization is filled with tons of successes. But the *con-*

sequences of success in an advancing organization are radically different from success in an oscillating organization. In structural advancement, success ultimately breeds long-term success; you can build on it, you can grow other successes, you can create momentum, energy and drive; in organizations in which structural oscillation rules the roost, success is only transitory.

Structural Advancement

There is one major telltale sign that an organization is advancing: its achievements are a platform for further achievements. For an organization that is advancing, everything counts; even those things that don't work are transformed into significant learning that eventually leads to success.

Advancement describes moving from somewhere to somewhere else. We throw a ball and it moves from our hand to where it lands, from one condition, to another.

In our organizations, we want our actions to move us from an actual state (the current situation), to a desired state (our goals and aspirations)—movement that *resolves* once we accomplish our goals.

The word *resolution* implies movement coming to an end. In the most effective organizations, there is example after example of resolving behavior. Action is first generated, then comes to an end once we achieve our goal. The path of least resistance leads us from the original desire for an outcome to its achievement.

Project teams complete assignments, write reports, prepare budgets, carry out advertising campaigns, and generate products. Management coordinates these various individual acts into an organizational tapestry of effective tactics and strategy. When done well, the organization's activities reinforce each other beautifully, leading to true alignment. Then the organization reaches a consistent level of high performance.

By building the right underlying structures that form an *advancing* path of least resistance, an organization is able to continually move ahead toward its next goal, and next goals after that. After all, that is the essence of the creative process in action. Something is created, and then, because it is created, it supports more and more future creations.

In this kind of organization, each person's actions count, contributing to the energy and talent of the entire enterprise. The company is engaged in a collective and collaborative creative process.

To almost anyone who has worked in a corporation, this situation sounds utopian.

Most organizations are not structured to bring out the best performance in their members or in the company itself. Organizations can seem dedicated to robbing people of their individuality, their unique character, and even their soul. Companies can seem to drift to pettiness, shortsightedness, and collective absurdities that can make you think that you've wandered into an insane asylum rather than the world of corporate professionalism. The best and most important creative competitive advantages can be lost on the powers-that-be. The pearls of the experience, talent, energy, dedication, and wisdom of the organizations' members can go untapped, unrecognized, and ignored. Why? Because the other type of behavior structure produces is *oscillation*.

Structural Oscillation versus Structural Advancement

The path of least resistance in structural oscillation moves from one place to another, but *then* moves back toward its original position. In an organization that oscillates, a period of advancement is followed by a reversal. Success and progress are nullified. The reversal within the structure is an inevitable product of the progress that came before it.

To demonstrate the difference between advancement and oscillation, I often use two of my daughter Eve's toys: a small Barbie car, and a doll's rocking chair.

First, I push the rocking chair forward. When I take my hand off it, the chair rocks backwards. I repeat this demonstration a few times, and a predictable pattern of behavior becomes obvious. Forward motion is followed by backward motion. The rocking chair rocks. Then I take Eve's bright red Barbie car and shoot it down the middle of the room. It usually comes to rest near the back of the room. The car moves from one place to another, and then stops.

The rocking chair is a good example of a structure that produces oscillation; the car is an example of advancement.

Next I take the car and place it in the seat of the rocking chair. I move the chair forward and then let it go. The result is like what happens in many organizations. No matter how much advancement has been accomplished, the organization still oscillates. While there are many things that succeed and advance, their success is neutralized by the more senior structure, the oscillation that is represented in my metaphor of the rocking chair. In this type of organization, success eventually doesn't succeed. This is the situation you may have experienced in your professional life when your great success didn't lead to more success, but was somehow lost in the shuffle.

Then I place the rocking chair on top of the car and push it. This is like an organization in which an advancing structure is dominant, even if it happens to contain some oscillating behavior. There may be pockets of oscillation, but the bigger influence is advancement. Another way to think of this is a rocking chair on a ship. The rocking chair may oscillate back and forth, but the ship is moving forward, carrying with it the rocking chair. In this type of advancing organization, you can make true progress and you can get where you want to go.

The rocking chair and the car demonstrate two different structures—two different paths of least resistances.

Although we want resolving behaviors that leads to advancement, progress, and ultimate success, too often we are plagued with chronic oscillating behavior that seems to keep pushing us back. Just like a rocking chair, once we move toward our goals, we appear to reach a crucial point in which something seems to move us away from where we want to be. Every step forward seems to cause a step back, and progress is eventually neutralized. What an exercise in frustration.

Why did our success eventually lead to difficulties? Why did opportunities turn into problems? Everyone has a plausible explanation, but these opinions cloud the real structural issue that caused things to happen the way they did. Some people love to point their fingers at the "villains" that blew it. They speculate about why growth led to downsizing or why they were caught by surprise by the competition's new product introduction or why their customers went elsewhere. Was it poor planning or bad leadership by senior management? Was it poor execution by the rank and file? Was it the international economy? Competition? The cost of labor? Unimaginative research and development? A weak marketing strategy? The boss's preoccupation with his or her golf game? The stars, dear Brutus?

Any or all of these factors might be present as symptoms, but they are not the cause. Most people, especially the ones who love to speculate, rarely ask, "What the heck caused these symptoms?"

The second inescapable law of organizational structure helps us understand what is going on.

The **SECOND** Law of Organizational Structure

In organizations that oscillate, success is neutralized. In organizations that advance, success succeeds.

How Oscillation Neutralizes Success

In an oscillating organization, individuals, teams, departments, and divisions may create success, but success in one department can cause trouble in other parts of the organization.

Increased sales can strain manufacturing capacity. New products can confuse buyers and lead to instability in established markets. Reinvestment can lead to declining stock market performance. The path of least resistance can lead people to compete against other people within the same organization more fiercely than against the real competition.

After five months of hard work, John and his team developed a new line of washbasins that were replicas of French sinks from the thirties. They were on time and within budget, and everyone thought their line of products was wonderful. This was seen as a big success for John and his team. They looked forward to the marketing campaign and the national distribution of their line. John and his team were "psyched."

Time passed, and John was assigned a new team of people to work with. More time passed, and John began to ask the folks in marketing when the new line would be coming out. "Never," was the response he got. "Why?" he asked. "Things change. No one likes French any-more," said his marketing colleague. "We need to get back to basics. That's what people want," said the marketing manager.

The company had made a decision to invest in a French-style line of plumbing supplies, but then later thought it was the wrong thing to do. In this case, success led to waste of resources and time. John thought he and his team succeeded, but in the end it failed to go anywhere.

Structural consultant Chloe Cox, of the British firm Strategy by Design, has described success leading to failure as a chronic behavior that she and her colleagues repeatedly confront:

> In the past we helped many teams accomplish their goals on time and within budget. But six months after the big success, and celebratory champagne, the accomplishments caused dilemmas in other parts of the organization. As a company, we decided to only do project planning or team development if we could be involved with the overall structure of the organization, or if the organization was well structured from the start. Otherwise, it is a waste of the client's money and our time.

Oscillation Camouflaged as Success

We are usually aware of the success we create, but we may not notice the aftermath of the success, which moves us away from the success we created. Success can camouflage oscillation for several reasons.

First, success is rewarded whether or not an organization is governed by structural oscillation or advancement. Almost universally, success is seen as a good thing, something we would like repeated again and again. Various rewards, such as bonuses, promotions, increased authority, and higher salaries come with success, whether or not success ultimately succeeds or fails. But the organization can seem so complex with so much going on, that it's hard to see the real story: that the path of least resistance leads first to success, but then away from it.

Second, for many organizations, some limited progress is made in spite of the oscillation. Small degrees of growth are squeezed out of the situation as people toil against the forces in play. Some rocking chairs actually move ahead after some amount of rocking. Two steps forward and one-and-three-quarter steps back does represent a type of movement. But at what cost?

Third, oscillation can take place over a long period of time, even years. When oscillation moves that slowly, it is not obvious that a structural pattern is in play. But if you look at the patterns in many organizations, every two or three years we are going in the opposite direction than we were two or three years before.

When we're busy with our problems, concerns, and the immediate demands we face, it's natural to focus on those factors. Who's got time to back up and look at the organization with a long-term perspective? And who in the organization has time to listen to your report if you did? Not many. We're all just too busy. This isn't wrong, but being this busy doesn't help.

Fourth, oscillation is disguised because at least half the time we're moving in the direction that we want to go. We make progress and we congratulate each other. We never see the reversal coming. We are taken by surprise when the pendulum shifts away from our successes. When a rocking chair moves forward, it must move back. It can only follow the path of least resistance.

During their periods of growth, the IBMs, the GMs, the DECs of the world seemed to enjoy unending success. How were they to know they were subject to oscillation? When the cycle changed, their profits declined and their markets weakened. The senior managers were vilified as if they had caused the problems. Had they? Or were they, too, the victims of an oscillating structure in which past success was bound to lead to future decline as the path of least resistance changed? Even leaders can be victims of an inadequate structure.

As the pendulum shifts again and the path of least resistance changes direction, and some of these companies begin to succeed again, we are left with a pretty good question: Have they truly shifted to structural advancement, or are they simply setting up their next major decline?

A Little Lesson in Structure

We are driving down the road, and we want to go straight ahead. But, the wheels of our car are out of alignment and the car pulls to the left. We compensate, and steer to the right. When we do, we can go straight.

This behavior, steering to the right, was our way of compensating for an inadequate structure. We are trying to do what we want—drive straight— but to do so, we need to take some unusual behavior.

One day our know-it-all friend comes with us. He notices our hands on the steering wheel. He hesitates to say anything for as long as he can stand it—two or three minutes. Finally, he says, "You know, you keep pulling the steering wheel to the right. Now, we've done many studies on the steering performances of successful drivers (he would have), and we find successful drivers steer straight when they are driving straight. So, if you want to be like other successful drivers, what you should do is steer in a straight line!" He then gets out of the car, because, like a lot of advice givers, he doesn't want to hang around and see the fruits of his advice. We try to take his advice and we steer straight like all of the good drivers he tested. In about twenty seconds, we steer to the right again. The underlying structure did not support the new process.

Steering straight is a good idea for a car with aligned wheels. There are many good practices that are good ideas if the company that is adopting them is well structured. But, if it's not well structured, the best idea in the world might hurt rather than help.

This story leads us to the third law of organizational structure.

> The **THIRD** Law of Organizational Structure
>
> ## If the organization's structure remains unchanged, the organization's behavior will revert to its previous behavior.

Michael Greenidge, a business process design manager for BC Telecom, described this situation that many organizations experience:

> Every time we go through some major organizational change, our executive managers find "tools" or methods to help. ABCM, reengineering, different process consultants bring in other methods—we implement them, but then we find half way

through the process the organization isn't taking them on. So then we abandon them, but later new tools are brought in. People are really up in the air about it all.

Is it any wonder that people easily slip into the role of house skeptics? Over the years, they have watched change effort after change effort hit their organizations and have seen excitement for each new system fade once the idea is put into practice. They have seen champions, systems, and mottoes come and go while the organization remains unchanged. Why should they "believe" when they have seen every attempt at change fail?

These people are forced to conclude that attempts at change are wasteful, that they take people away from the company's real work, and, therefore, they may even be distracting and harmful.

Changing Structure

If we took the car to a garage and got the wheels aligned, our steering habits would change immediately. When we wanted to drive straight, we would steer straight. And it wouldn't take any time to adopt the new behavior. In this case, a change of structure leads to a change of behavior automatically and naturally. This, in fact, is the fourth law of organizational structure.

> The FOURTH Law of Organizational Structure
>
> **A change of structure leads to a change of the organization's behavior.**

Just what kind of change of structure would help the organization move from an oscillating to an advancing pattern? That is the subject of the next chapter!

Quick Review

Structure and Structural Laws

- A structure is an entity made up of individual elements that impact one another by the relationships they form.

- Organizations follow the path of least resistance through inescapable structural laws.

- Understanding these laws will enable us to understand why organizations behave the way they do and how we can redesign them to perform the way we want.

Organizational Advancement and Oscillation

The first law of organizational structure is: Organizations either oscillate or advance.

- Advancement means moving from where we are to where we want to be. Oscillation means moving from where we are toward where we want to be, but then moving back to the original position.

- The second law of organizational structure is: In organizations that oscillate, success is neutralized. In ones that advance, success succeeds.

- When success succeeds, one success breeds a chain of further successes. When success is neutralized, success is short term or ephemeral.

- Since oscillating movement can take place over a long period of time, and some of that time the organization is moving in the direction it wants to go, oscillating patterns are often hard to see.

- Understanding the nature of structure is essential for an organization to redesign itself so that it can change the path of least resistance from oscillation to advancement.

- If the organization's structure remains unchanged, the organization's behavior will revert to its previous behavior. That's the third law of organizational structure.

- A change of structure leads to a change of the organization's behavior. That's the fourth law of organizational structure.

Structural Tension

The Secret of Your Success

What words are to language, what numbers are to mathematics, or what the feedback loop is to system dynamics, tension is to structure. It is the basic unit. It is like an energy cell that fuels movement and change. It is the factor in structure that forms the path of least resistance.

The word *tension* has a few different meanings, so let's be clear about what we mean and don't mean by it. We *don't* mean emotional stress and anxiety. We *don't* mean pressure. We *don't* mean pain and suffering. We *do* mean a dynamic of structure that causes energy to move along the path of least resistance.

What Is Tension?

Tension is formed by discrepancy, or the difference between one thing and another.

Let's take a simple example of thirst. What is thirst anyway? There is a difference between how much liquid the body needs and how much it actually has at the moment. The path of least resistance created by the tension is to take action to end the difference, in other words, to drink. (When we're thirsty, it's easier to drink than not to drink.) Once we drink, we get rid of the difference between the desired state and the actual state. Our body has the same amount of liquid it desires. Then the tension is resolved, and the path of least resistance is to stop drinking. And we do.

This illustrates another key point: Tension wants to resolve.

Whenever we have a tension, such as thirst, hunger, or suspense, we want to resolve it. We do so by taking action, for example, drink, eat, find out "who done it." The tension itself strives for resolution. Once we have a tension, we have something that wants to resolve, or move away from the original situation to a different situation.

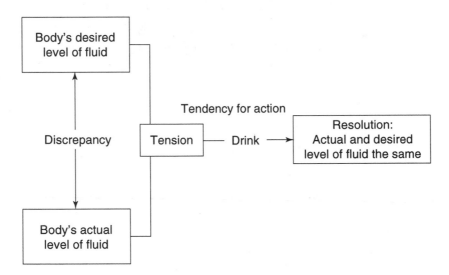

In this simple example, we can observe some of the most important principles about tension:

1. Tension is formed by a discrepancy or difference between two elements.

2. Tension creates a tendency for movement by forming a path of least resistance.

3. Tension resolves when the discrepancy ends.

Tension and Equilibrium

Tension creates a state of *nonequilibrium*. In our thirst example, the desired amount of water is not equal to the actual amount of water.

When a state of nonequilibrium exists within a structure, the structure attempts to restore equilibrium.

Thirst represents nonequilibrium between the actual amount of water and the desired amount of water. Equilibrium is created by drinking until the desired and actual amounts are the same.

Some people glorify equilibrium. But by itself, equilibrium is neither good nor bad. The same can be said for states of nonequilibrium. Being thirsty or not being thirsty is neither good nor bad; it merely reflects the state of tension within the body's biological system.

Let's now see how tension can be applied to organizations.

What Is Structural Tension?

Here is one of the major points in this book. The most important tension we will use in our redesign work is the difference between what we want and what we have—our desired state as compared to our actual state. The term for this type of tension is *structural tension*.

Structural Tension

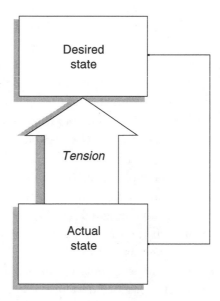

In all of our business and managerial design work with clients, structural tension is at the foundation of their planning and implementation success. Once we have established our desired end results and defined current reality in relationship to the end result, we have formed a tension that will be resolved by the action plan we create.

I can't say this strongly enough. This principle of structural tension—*knowing what we want to create and knowing where we are in relationship to our goals*—is the most powerful force an organization can have.

But it can sound too simple—and in a way it is too simple. Too simple to say, too simple to hear, so simple that it's easy to dismiss it, underestimate it, not quite get it, but think that we've gotten it.

It is easy to say: know what we want, know where we are, and develop a plan to get from here to there. But the actuality is hard, very hard. Let's now examine more closely both the pitfalls and the importance of the three elements of structural tension: defining our goals, defining where we are now, and taking action to reach our goals.

Goals That Fit and Goals That Don't

Many companies do not know what they want. That's not to say that they don't have goals. But, too often, when we look at the goals, they do not form a consistent pattern. The major goals don't fit together. In fact, often they are in conflict or they contradict each other. They haven't been well thought out, and they are filled with conflicts of interests. Organizations that "know" their goals are in a better position than companies that don't.

And the real test of whether an organization knows its goals comes when we look throughout the entire company. Do the various departments' and divisions' goals support each other, or are they in conflict with each other? Do people compete against each other for the same resources base—money, personnel, equipment—or is the organization's capacity logically designed to support the various activities needed to accomplish the overriding goals of the company? Is there a conflict between the goals of the financial people and the goals of the managers and business people within the organization? Are there conflicts between the product developers and the marketers? or do they work in coordination with each other?

In addition, every organization has lots of goals, but do people really know the goals, and, furthermore, do they understand why they are attempting to create these goals? The answer can be no.

A company's goals can be all over the map as you move from department to department. Goals created on local levels of the organization may have little to do with goals created on the corporate level. Dr. Jay Merluzzi, director of immunological diseases for Boehringer Ingelheim, has seen this happen among the new scientists who join an organization. The goals that they develop may not fit into the corporate direction. So, Dr. Merluzzi sets up structural tension with them, so their goals begin to fit into the overall direction of the organization. Here's how he described the situation:

> Many young scientists who come to industry find themselves as managers of laboratories and groups. In most cases, scientists have the talent, intellectual capability and knowledge to accomplish technical goals. But sometimes the science gets clouded . . . by a lack of wisdom. I have found that scientists can easily define the end-result of a scientific goal but they are not as adept at seeing the organizational goals that are needed to reach the technical target. As a technical/professional manager, I have found that setting up strong structural tension around well-defined organizational goals results in movement technically where there was little or none before. It is extremely effective.

The Critical Importance of Linking Goals

When we build our organizations on structural tension, goals have a special function—they are the prime organizing principles of the organization. Every action we take is linked to other goals that are linked to still other goals. And there is a very special way that goals are linked. They move from goals that reflect the overall purpose of the organization, to goals that reflect its business strategy, to goals that reflect the management strategy, and goals on the local level that support the management strategy.

The Relatedness of Goals

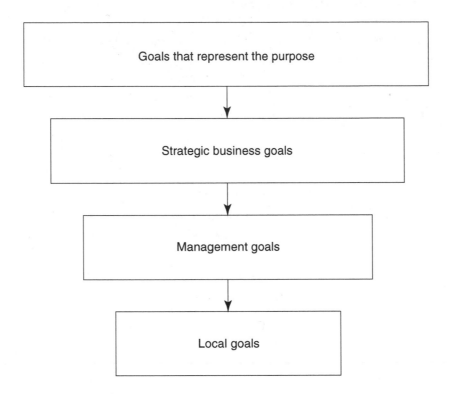

Goals that represent the purpose

Strategic business goals

Management goals

Local goals

When people on the local levels of the organization make up their own goals, they often don't always mesh with the goals other members of the organization have created. Goals may clash, setting up a situation where various groups must fight it out just to get adequate resources so they can do their jobs. Eventually, some win and some lose in a "survival of the fittest," goal-eat-goal world. What is absent in these types of situations is a true organizing principle that ties together all the goals, as well as everyone's energies and talents.

If we are to create a structural tension that leads an organization to advance rather than oscillate, we need to define our overriding end results, or our senior goals. Then we must make sure that all the other goals support those larger goals.

The senior goals define the overall direction of the company. Every other goal is the child of a parent goal, right up to these major organizational goals. Therefore, each goal has a *strategic* function. In this situation, an organization can truly advance because that is the path of least resistance.

One common characteristic in organizations that oscillate is that there is a shotgun approach toward goal setting. People try to have as many goals as they can think of, not because they know where they want to go, but in the hope that, if they do enough, some of it will stick.

Most organizations are not rich enough to succeed at that game— and if they were, they would be at a definite disadvantage from any competitors who were structured to advance. Any success that a shotgun approach may achieve will be neutralized in an oscillating structure. Without a vision of a clear end result, it is impossible to create structural tension. We will explore constructing highly workable end results later in Part 1 of this book.

Defining Reality Precisely

Then we come to the skill of defining reality precisely: Where are we in relationship to our goals? Managers need to learn how to observe reality objectively. We need the news and not the editorial. But not only that, we need to look at reality from a broader perspective than we are used to. We usually look at reality from our neck of the woods, but that's not a big enough perspective to get the entire picture. We need to get into a helicopter, and go straight up, and look at the whole woods. How do the parts fit together, or how do they not fit together? Without this perceptive insight, we will have trouble getting a fix on reality.

One of the most useful books I read when I first started a company said that most businesses go out of business within their first two years because of one thing, and one thing alone: bad accounting. Why? Because bad accounting doesn't give people a true fix on reality. They make decisions predicated on wrong information. They don't have a fix on one of the important aspects of reality, and so, they blow it.

Reality is, however, an acquired taste. Sometimes it is filled with pain, disappointment, and frustration. Sometimes it proves that our firm beliefs do not hold up to scrutiny. Sometimes reality can seem confusing. But, without becoming truly fluent in it, we mistakenly think we know all there is to know, and we make the wrong decisions. If we are to establish real structural tension, the current state of reality in relationship to the desired state must be well known and articulated.

Why is defining current reality often so hard? Because in most organizations, people distort reality. Mistakes are hidden. It's uncommon to see a report that says, "Hey Boss, I want you to know that I really screwed up!" It's more common for success to be exaggerated, and for people to ignore the obvious. People get rewarded for the good, not the bad, so who wants to talk about the bad.

A Little Lesson in Reality: Seeing What's Really There

Arthur Stern, a wonderful artist and teacher, makes this point in his book *Color—How to See and Paint It*: "Many painters don't paint what they see, but what they expect to see, what they think they see, what they remember, or what they imagine things are supposed to look like."

Stern tells the story of taking a group of his students to Riverside Park to look across the Hudson at New Jersey. He pointed to three architectural structures: an apartment house at the top of the Palisades; a storage tank down at the waterside; and a tall factory further up the river.

He then asked, "What color are those buildings?"

His students all gave him the same answers. The apartments were red. ("Red brick," someone said.) The storage tanks were white. And the factory was orange.

But then Stern handed around some small cards, each with a hole punched through it. He calls them spot screens. When people look through these cards at the objects in question, the color can be isolated, and seen out of context of the objects themselves. Once his students had the cards, he asked them to look through the hole.

"Now tell me what colors you see," Stern instructed his students. They became silent until finally one of them spoke up. "They're all blue, like the rest of the scenery over there when you look through the hole in the card." The other students joined in agreement. The red apartment house, the white tank, and the orange factory building all looked blue.

On hazy days, when we look off at the distant mountains, or across a river, or even down a long street, there is atmosphere between us and the distant objects. The atmosphere reflects light, often the light of the sky. That's why faraway mountains can look purple or blue. When the students isolated the color from the context of the buildings in question, they were forced to see what was really there. And they easily saw it, because it was there to see in objective reality.

In fact, it was always there to see, but they simply did not see what was before their eyes. Why not? Because they had a concept of what colors they thought they should see. They compared reality—the various buildings as they actually looked—to their notion of how these buildings should look. They ignored the information that didn't fit in with their notions. They happened to share the same concepts, so it was easy for them to agree about red, white, and orange.

Is this a trick of the mind, or is it that the mind works perfectly well for what it does, but we don't always happen to give it accurate information? In the Stern example, he knew his students were capable of seeing the actual color they were observing. That is why he brought the spot screen cards with him as part of his teaching approach. And, in fact, once they looked more precisely, the students could see what was there to see. But we must take a lesson from how they thought before they were given the cards.

People often substitute a concept of reality for reality. They then impose their concept on themselves.

Since one of the fundamentals of structural tension is an accurate view of reality, it is important to learn how to look freshly, rather than impose our old concepts on reality. Sherlock Holmes said to Watson, "You look, but you do not observe." Sometimes we're all Watson. We need to be Holmes.

When you look at reality, start without a concept, and you will be able to see more. Instead of filling what we don't know by speculating, just describe what you do know. As TV's *Dragnet*'s Sergeant Friday used to say, "Just the facts, Ma'am." If you separate what you know as fact from other than fact (speculations, conjecture, theories, concepts) you will see more reality, because when you don't know, you will ask. And that's a good thing.

There is a story of a man who was catching mice. One night he ran out of cheese for his mouse trap. So he left a picture of a big piece of cheese in the trap. In the morning he found he had caught a picture of a mouse.

A picture of a mouse is not a mouse, and a concept of reality is not reality.

We have been trained to see the world through the lens of our theories, experiences, ideals, worldviews, opinions, and speculations. This lens can distort reality, which will weaken or even destroy structural tension. Observing reality objectively is another discipline we will explore both later in Part 1 of this book, as well as in Part 3.

And Now, Taking Action

Once we establish structural tension by defining a desired end result and defining an organization's current reality, we are ready to create and implement our action plans. But these action plans aren't any old action plans. They are created in the context of structural tension. They form the path of least resistance, the path that moves most naturally from our starting point to our ending point. Actions taken within the structural context of structural tension are easier to take than ones that are not formed in that context. They tend to be better, more precise, and more efficient and effective.

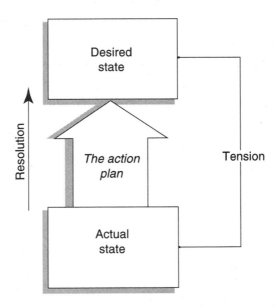

What are the steps we must take in moving from here to there? Within the form of structural tension, highly effective and practical plans can be tailor-made. But making these plans is not simply "filling in the gap" as I have sometimes heard it erroneously described.

A gap suggests an empty space between something and something else. Instead of an empty space (the absence of something) there is a tension (the presence of a powerful dynamic force). Tension, as a dynamic force, seeks resolution. One way we begin to resolve the tension is by designing action plans. Another way is by implementing these plans.

If you've been a manager who has had to force your people into action or had to manipulate an uncooperative system, you haven't been using structural tension. You must define the right goals for you and your team, and each of you must be fluent in these goals. Understand why these goals are important and how they relate to the rest of the organization's goals.

You and your people must track reality as it is and as it changes. You may need to create faster systems for gathering intelligence, to get the news on time rather than when it's too late to do anything about it.

Once these important factors are in place, you can design an action plan that is practical, because it takes into account clear goals and the real situation you are starting from. You will update current reality as it changes and update your action plans as needed. But you will not have to push against an uncooperative system. Instead, you will be building a new structure in which the path of least resistance is to take the actions you have designed, when you need to take them. This ups your chances of getting where you want to go.

Organizations in Which Structural Tension Is Dominant

In organizations in which structural tension is dominant, people can be accurate and objective about reality, and they can tell each other what they see. They explore differences of opinion and observation, and they help each other clarify the actual state in relation to the desired state. When this is the case, strategies and action plans can be evaluated and adjusted based on true learning, rather than as reactions against conflicts and problems.

In organizations structured to advance, actions lead to evaluations, which lead to adjustments, which lead to other actions. People get innovative and creative as they develop processes to help them get where they want to go.

Any process is only as good as the results it produces. Only when we understand just what the process needs to accomplish can we truly reinvent and redesign it. John Teti, vice-chairman of the La France Corporation (a medium-sized manufacturing company that is a supplier for Hewlett-Packard, Ford Motors, Tandy, and others) put it like this:

> I don't think our process planning was very efficient when we started to use a structural approach. But when we started applying it, we didn't say anything to anyone. We didn't give it any grand introduction. We just started using it, and what it did immediately was eliminate a lot of talk about irrelevant things. When we started talking about what any particular goal was, and clarified reality, our planning time was cut by a third.

And La France's Executive Vice President George Barrar said:

> By using a structural approach, we got an awful lot of insights into the business that we wouldn't normally have gotten. I think from a process planning standpoint one of the big improvements is [that] before we did a lot of fluff.

When any management process comes into vogue, the fad makes it easy for people to forget the point of the actions they are taking. This often happens when people search for the best practices and for improved efficiency without tying these activities to their specific goals. What does the process serve? There is nothing wrong with wanting better processes or studying the methods others have used. But too often people get lost. Without knowing our goals and current reality, how could we know if the changes in process really worked? We wouldn't. So it's important to establish and work with structural tension throughout the organization.

Here is the fifth inescapable law of organization structure:

The **FIFTH** Law of Organizational Structure

When structural tension dominates an organization, the organization will advance.

In an organization where structural tension is the dominant structure, a structural approach is built in companywide, and the organization's path of least resistance is to advance. Swedforest, an international forestry consulting company with headquarters in Sweden, is such an organization. Jerker Thunberg, Swedforest's managing director, recently talked about his company's experience with using the structural approach:

> During the two years Swedforest has worked with structural approach, most of our staff and managers, as well as administrative and support staff, have been involved in defining what we want to be and what results we want to achieve. The structural approach, building strategies taking you toward the desired results, is an enormously powerful tool for change and management. The realization of the structural tension between desired end results and current reality has given us energy to start changing the organization to achieve the results we want. Swedforest is not the same company as it was two years ago and the most fascinating and positive thing is that once you start working with the structural approach there is no way back to the old problem-solving, situational thinking that is so self-defeating. We become more and more effective and successful. I can only wish that many more companies would start to learn and apply a structural approach in managing themselves.

As La France's John Teti put it, "People get sensitized to structural tension, and they recognize what works and what doesn't work. The logic never leaves them. The actions they take are never arbitrary. They can learn right away, and help each other learn too."

John Wolverton, an internal structural consultant and program manager at the United States Air Force's Wright Laboratory, sees the use of structural tension as the key factor in expanding managerial excellence across the organization:

> I've had the privilege of working with only a few really great managers in my life. What fascinated me the most was their ability to consistently produce results, no matter what the issues were. I've been looking most of my life for that principle or key process they possessed that others didn't. Now, based on my work with the structural approach, it is obvious what the key is. It is structural tension. I can't imagine managing a project any other way now.

Katherine Freeman, director of Riverside Methodist Hospital's Alcohol and Drug Dependency department, reports that the use of structural tension in her organization has led to a new pattern of success:

> After we did our first training in the structural approach back in 1993, we were able to create remarkable results. Ten or twelve years prior to that, director after director had the same issues and had really never much achieved any end results that they wanted, certainly never had any financial results. There was a lot of talk about management strategy, but it wasn't working. Over a three-year period we completely restructured the clinical program using structural tension, and aligning all the pieces. We ended up last year with better patient outcomes, less recidivism than ever before and made the strongest and only contribution to the bottom line in the history of the department. And we ended up with incredibly high morale. To the physicians in behavioral health, this was a miracle. They started to want to know what happened in our department that caused our success.

The difference between our goals and current reality forms a powerful tension, and when we set up a tension in an organization, people can join together to resolve it. And this resolution advances the organization, even when the organization is governmental. Jeffery Arnold, a structural consultant from Montreal, has reported how structural tension was used by a township in Quebec Province.

> In the early days of my involvement with the structural approach, I was a councilor on the municipal government of a rural township. The Quebec provincial government mandated that all municipal governments have an urban plan with accompanying bylaws.
>
> We began a complex two year process by describing a vision of the municipality and then describing current reality. This established structural tension, which carried us through an iterative process of finding resources, advice and counsel, developing the plan, public consultations and government approvals. This process resulted in a legal framework that has maintained the integrity of the resident's collective vision for the Township.
>
> The urban plan has stood the test of time and some serious challenges over the many years it has been in place. In one instance, residents of the township were able to successfully defend against the concerted effort of a large multinational to

establish an enormous dump in the municipality which would have had very negative impact on the quality of life and property values. Not only that, we were able to build more and more of the quality of life we wanted over extended periods of time.

Never underestimate how absolutely powerful structural tension is. It is a generative structure in which the path of least resistance leads toward the successful achievement of our goals.

How do you use structural tension? That is the subject of the next few chapters. We will learn the basics and about the powerful technique of Structural Tension Charting, so we can design our organizations to succeed brilliantly.

Quick Review

- Tension is created by a difference between two related elements.

- Once a tension exists, it creates a tendency to move toward resolution, generating the path of least resistance. The basic unit of structure is the tension-resolution system.

- Structural tension—the desired state in relation to the actual state—is the key ingredient in organizations that advance.

- Structural tension produces advancement in an organization because of the organizational behaviors that it promotes: goals are interrelated, reality is seen objectively, and adjustments to plans and organizational learning become the norm.

- The Fifth Law of Organizational Structure is: When structural tension dominates an organization, the organization will advance.

Structural Tension Charting
The Key to Organizational Design

There is nothing more powerfully generative for an organization's success than using structural tension as its primary organizing principle. All successful companies use it—some very consciously, some with "unconscious competence." The more consciously an organization can use structural tension, the more it can control its own destiny.

The primary technique for creating structural tension within organizations is *Structural Tension Charting*. In Structural Tension Charting, identifying our major goals becomes the driving force for defining our current reality and creating our action plan to reach those goals.

Charting can be used by senior management in a top-down approach. It can also be used within teams, departments, and divisions. Individuals can use it for their professional and personal work, as well.

Let's begin by looking at Structural Tension Charting in a top-down approach within organizations.

Top-Down Design

Organizations that use a top-down approach in forming structural tension have a distinct advantage over companies that don't. These organizations truly know their overriding goals and they are fluent in reality. Their actions support each other, which in turn builds tremendous momentum.

Structural Tension Charting helps us "compose" the organization like great orchestral music. The goals that we form, like the themes and sub-themes in music, are based on our purpose as an organization and our business strategy.

Using our business strategy as a platform, we can form specific goals that reflect the strategy. If, for example, our business strategy were based on lowest price to the customer, on-time delivery, and adequate quality, our goals would reflect that. Our goals would reflect a cost structure and levels of managerial efficiency that would lead to our products having the lowest price possible. Our goals would also set the right standards of quality, and they would reinforce the appropriate delivery goals. (We will explore the deep waters of business strategy in Chapter 11.)

Whatever the business strategy is, our goals need to be consistent with it.

Identifying Our Overriding Goals

An organization needs to have clear overriding major goals. Goals give us direction, and overriding goals give the entire organization direction. If we didn't have overriding goals, we would not be able to coordinate everyone's focus in a common direction. So, the goals must be clear to everyone.

An overriding goal may include various aspects of our business. Let's say that our business success depends on new product releases, and we need to have at least seven new product releases a year for us to stay competitive. Then, *seven product releases per year* becomes our goal. By when might we accomplish our goal? Let's say that we need to accomplish that level of new product releases by two years from now.

Once we have determined what we want, everyone can understand exactly what the goal is: seven new products released annually.

Even if, at the time of conceiving the goal, we don't know what these seven products may be, the goal is clear. The due date is also clear.

> **7 new product introductions per year (by year 2)**

Now that we know our goal, we have accomplished the first step in the Structural Tension Charting process. The next step is to define our current status of our goal. We call this *current reality*.

Defining Current Reality

Because our goal deals with new product releases, what is our current reality in that area? Let's say we now introduce three new products a year. What else might we need to describe in current reality to better define our starting point? Perhaps it's that we have two product development teams, they share the same facility, it's hard to hire new people for product development because the job market has higher demand than supply, and so on. We position the goal in relationship to current reality so we can see the *difference*. Remember that this difference is what creates the wonderfully useful tension that will energize our process. As managers, we will "hold" the tension throughout our creative process as we work toward accomplishing our result.

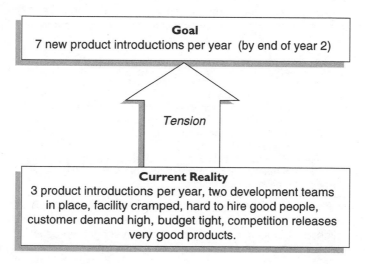

Goal
7 new product introductions per year (by end of year 2)

Tension

Current Reality
3 product introductions per year, two development teams
in place, facility cramped, hard to hire good people,
customer demand high, budget tight, competition releases
very good products.

Creating an Action Plan

After we have defined our goals and described our current reality, we have established structural tension. We have set up a path of least resistance in which energy is more likely to flow in the direction of the successful release of seven new products a year than anywhere else. But simply sitting around the organization meditating on structural tension will do very little to help us reach our goals. We need to take action. And we can take more effective action if we have a plan mapped out. So, our next step is to write an action plan by writing in the steps we need to take to reach our goal.

In the process of Structural Tension Charting, there is a special way to develop detail. The technique we use is called *telescoping*. Telescoping will be extensively discussed in Chapter 4, but, briefly, it involves creating charts on which broad action steps are described, and these steps generate other charts in which the details to accomplish each step are worked out.

So, the first level of description for our example chart will be very broad indeed, and this will help us work from larger shapes first to various levels of details later. This is an important thought process, because it helps us see the details in relationship with the overview, rather than get lost in them.

So here is our example structural tension chart as we add an overall action plan:

Goal: 7 new product introductions per year (by end of year 2)

- Streamline prototype testing process
- Increase product introductions to five by year 1
- Create two new development teams
- Create and implement subcontractor process
- Hire six more product development professionals
- Work out alliance with Marketing
- Expand facility
- Work out costs and rebudget Product Group
- Streamline and implement new product development system

Current Reality: 3 product introductions per year, two development teams in place, facility cramped, hard to hire good people, customer demand high, budget tight, competition releases very good products.

This is how we form a Structural Tension Chart for one of our major organizational goals.

Gloria Cosgrove, director of regulatory training, and an in-house structural consultant for Boehringer Pharmaceutical, has described what it is like when using structural tension with the groups she works with:

> From a management point of view, the people working with me are extremely focused in terms of where they are going and where they are. They are involved in the thought process, and there is a very different energy in the group when we're using Structural Tension Charting. Everyone is all on the same track, and they really understand it. Not just the work, but they really understand the thought process—how things fit together, how they work as a whole.

The example above shows the basics of Structural Tension Charting, but obviously organizations have more than one goal. Let's now create a chart that includes all of the organization's major goals—what's called a *Master Structural Tension Chart*.

Charting in a Top-Down Approach—The Master Plan

There are many ways of planning, many of them very good. The idea behind planning is to organize our thinking first and then our actions second. When our plans are translated into structural tension charts, we can better describe our goals, our understanding of reality, and our overall action strategy. Work very broadly at first, and then, later, develop details from the overall shape of our plan.

From insights about how our particular business works, we can generate overall goals. These goals include many dimensions of our business focus—financial results, marketing results, sales results, product development results, customer satisfaction goals, response time goals, organizational goals, market share goals, and so on, might be included in our goal setting process. Here is an example of an organization's master goal:

> **$675 million in sales, 15% profit, 7 new product introductions a year, we are in 36 countries, 35% market share (U.S.), average of 25% market share outside U.S., adequate capacity in all areas, 2 new business opportunities, the organization has high morale and is aligned, perfect safety record.**

Now that we have defined our goal, it's time to describe its current reality. Each element on our master goal list will need something in the current reality box, and we will add other relevant information to get an essential picture of reality.

> $412 million in sales, 12% profit, 3 new product introductions a year, we are in 21 countries, 25% market share (U.S.), average of 15% market share outside U.S., capacity strained in some areas, haven't pursued new business opportunities, the organization has okay morale but is sometimes unaligned, 2 safety problems this past year. The market is growing at 12% a year, we have 3 major competitors who are the same size and 15 or so small competitors that chip away at us, we have the highest product quality, we have 85% on-time delivery which is unacceptable to our distributors, we have access to capital, our management systems are out of date, we have very good IT systems, our core competencies are a major competitive advantage, we have useless delays in making our decisions. We understand our business strategy, which works well.

Once structural tension is defined, we are ready to write our broadly described action plan. The action plan will contain several focuses, including product development, R&D, marketing, sales, management, the development of capacity, capital, manufacturing, and so on.

Goal: $675 million in sales, 15% profit, 7 new product introductions a year, we are in 36 countries, 35% market share (U.S.), average of 25% market share outside U.S., adequate capacity in all areas, 2 new business opportunities, the organization has high morale and is aligned, perfect safety record.

- **Update all patents/new patents**
- **Add needed capacity**
- **Develop 2 new business opportunities**
- **Target 14 new countries and begin doing business there**
- **Create/implement R&D strategy**
- **Update all internal management systems**
- **Improve shipping system for 100% on-time delivery**
- **Design and implement new marketing/sales strategy**

Current Reality: $412 million in sales, 12% profit, 3 new product introductions a year, we are in 21 countries, 25% market share (U.S.), average of 15% market share outside U.S., capacity strained in some areas, haven't pursued new business opportunities, the organization has okay morale but is sometimes unaligned, 2 safety problems this past year. The market is growing at 12% a year, we have 3 major competitors who are the same size and 15 or so small competitors that chip away at us, we have the highest product quality, we have 85% on-time delivery which is unacceptable to our distributors, we have access to capital, our management systems are out of date, we have very good IT systems, our core competencies are a major competitive advantage, we have useless delays in making our decisions. We understand our business strategy, which works well.

Due Dates and Accountability

Once we have defined the end result we want, the current reality we have, and our action plans, the next step is to assign due dates and accountability.

The due dates are quite a significant part of the planning process. Through the assignment of dates, you are placing events in time.

Of course, the major due date is for the master chart. Is it to be accomplished within two years? Three years? Five years?

Once we know that, we can assign dates to our action steps. Some actions can't be accomplished until other actions are accomplished. The materials have to arrive at the factory before they can be made into the product. The product has to be made before it can be shipped, and so on. Some actions are not as dependent on other actions, and their due date doesn't drive other due dates.

When the groups I have worked with got to the point of setting dates, there was a distinct change in the energy and seriousness that took place. At first, the charting process may have seemed like an academic exercise. The more filled in the chart was, the more reality it took on. Adding the dates produced another level of the reality and the do-ability of the process. People begin to see just what it would take to reach their goals—not only what actions would be necessary, but also how those actions would play themselves out over time.

Goal: $675 million in sales, 15% profit, 7 new product introductions a year, we are in 36 countries, 35% market share (U.S.), average of 25% market share outside U.S., adequate capacity in all areas, 2 new business opportunities, the organization has high morale and is aligned, perfect safety record.

• Update all patents/new patents	12/15
• Add needed capacity	10/30
• Develop 2 new business opportunities	9/18
• Target 14 new countries and begin doing business there	7/25
• Create/implement R&D strategy	6/1
• Update all internal management systems	5/15
• Improve shipping system for 100% on-time delivery	4/15
• Design and implement new marketing/ sales strategy	3/1

Current Reality: $412 million in sales, 12% profit, 3 new product introductions a year, we are in 21 countries, 25% market share (U.S.), average of 15% market share outside U.S., capacity strained in some areas, haven't pursued new business opportunities, the organization has okay morale but is sometimes unaligned, 2 safety problems this past year. The market is growing at 12% a year, we have 3 major competitors who are the same size and 15 or so small competitors that chip away at us, we have the highest product quality, we have 85% on-time delivery which is unacceptable to our distributors, we have access to capital, our management systems are out of date, we have very good IT systems, our core competencies are a major competitive advantage, we have useless delays in making our decisions. We understand our business strategy, which works well.

The next step in the process is to assign accountabilities to the various action steps. Who is going to be accountable to making sure the action is completed? The rule of thumb is to assign only one person as accountable, rather than a group or more than one person. Accountable doesn't mean that you are the one who has to do all of the work. It means that you are the manager of the action step, and your job is to see to it that the step is accomplished. Usually you do this by involving other people.

Goal: $675 million in sales, 15% profit, 7 new product introductions a year, we are in 36 countries, 35% market share (U.S.), average of 25% market share outside U.S., adequate capacity in all areas, 2 new business opportunities, the organization has high morale and is aligned, perfect safety record.

• Update all patents/new patents	12/15	RD
• Add needed capacity	10/30	FG
• Develop 2 new business opportunities	9/18	RD
• Target 14 new countries and begin doing business there	7/25	GH
• Create/implement R&D strategy	6/1	HJ
• Update all internal management systems	5/15	MK
• Improve shipping system for 100% on-time delivery	4/15	FG
• Design and implement new marketing/ sales strategy	3/1	HJ

Current Reality: $412 million in sales, 12% profit, 3 new product introductions a year, we are in 21 countries, 25% market share (U.S.), average of 15% market share outside U.S., capacity strained in some areas, haven't pursued new business opportunities, the organization has okay morale but is sometimes unaligned, 2 safety problems this past year. The market is growing at 12% a year, we have 3 major competitors who are the same size and 15 or so small competitors that chip away at us, we have the highest product quality, we have 85% on-time delivery which is unacceptable to our distributors, we have access to capital, our management systems are out of date, we have very good IT systems, our core competencies are a major competitive advantage, we have useless delays in making our decisions. We understand our business strategy, which works well.

As we develop the process of structural tension charting, we will see how the accountable person can use other structural tension charts to more easily manage the entire process of accomplishing the assignments.

The Master Structural Tension Chart

Structural Tension Charting may consist of a single chart that shows the end result as contrasted with the current reality, and actions that are designed to accomplish the goal.

It may also consist of several related structural tension charts that develop the overall goal, first in a broad-brush level of description, and later in more and more details. (More about this in the next chapter.)

The first structural tension chart for an organization is called *The Master Chart*, because it will contain all of the major goals over a period of time, perhaps one or two years or more, depending on what makes sense for the organization or industry. The accomplishment of these goals on the Master Chart represents a major milestone in the organization's development and growth.

Using Structural Tension Charting for Project Team

Another powerful use of structural tension charting is in the project team or management team. In this situation, the team goes through the same steps. They define the goal that they are assigned to create. Then they describe the goal's current reality. And then they define the action steps.

The difference between structural tension charting on the team level rather than the whole organization level is that only the project team is involved in their planning work—commonly ten to twelve members, more or less. By using the structural tension charting process, everyone, and especially the project manager, can create an economy of means.

Structural Tension Charting does more than simply organize work in a logical way. It also changes the group dynamics and energy. The underlying structure supports the path of least resistance, moving directly toward the accomplishment of the project, and the structural tension itself generates energy as it moves toward resolution. This creates momentum within the work team, and as actions are completed, there is a growing forward moving force that makes it easier to take the next actions.

Goal: Release of the model TZx56.2 1/15		
• Beta-test	11/15	UH
• Alpha-test and adjust	9/1	JH
• Test new code	8/12	HU
• Write new code	8/1	DT
• Update TZx55.5	7/19	FC
• Subcontract developers to work on TTx technology	7/16	UH
• Write specs	7/1	DT
• Design new features as add-ons	6/24	JH

Current Reality: The TZx55.5 has been on the market for over a year, people want three more features to help in their cellular use of it when interfacing with other systems.

The mental landscape also changes. Rather than the mental turmoil that often happens around high-energy teams, there is a focus and mental clarity. The experience is getting all extraneous things off your mind, and having the breadth and depth of a lucid mind. And the group sees the wider structural relationship among the various parts, and they better understand the relevance of the work they do.

Using Structural Tension Charting for Individuals

The use of structural tension charting is not limited to groups. You can use it in with your own projects or workload. We all suffer from being human, which means that we tend to have a lot on our mind. We think, fret, ponder, obsess, and dwell on thousands of details everyday. In this over-information age, we are given too much information that isn't that useful. Much of it is a waste of time.

By disciplining our thought process, we can gain better focus and effectiveness. Our thought process is helped by a similar principle that Mark Twain used when talking about the amount of cigars he smoked. He said, "I make it a point to only smoke one cigar . . . (pause) . . . at a time." In charting, we can learn to only consider one topic area . . . at a time.

Before we start to speculate on what might happen, how to figure out what we should do, why it got to be that way, who you need to contact, etc., ask, "What am I trying to create?" or "What is the result I am after?"

If you don't know what you're after, it will make it harder for you to create it! Running around like a chicken with its head cut off doesn't up your chances of success. You need the discipline to know the result you want and the situation you have. Anytime, no matter how fast-paced or how pressured the circumstances, you can take a moment out of the craziness, and ask yourself, "What do I want?" and "Where am I now?"

Until you know the answers to those questions, many of your efforts may be useless. You can feel that you're flying close to the ground at Mach 1 without a destination. Once you know where you want to go and where you are now, you become as focused as Robin Hood aiming an arrow.

Recently, my wife Rosalind and I were flying back from an eight-hour meeting. Our heads were swimming with all the things that we had to do. As time passed, we got more and more frenetic. We then said to each other, "Why don't we do a structural tension chart?" And we pulled out the old laptop and began to locate the end result we wanted, our current reality, and then we put together an action plan. Within fifteen minutes, we were changed people—calm, clear, happy, productive, and in love. (Okay, we were in love before we did the structural tension charting but it sure is nice to create together.)

Charting and Your Personal Life

To help deepen the experience of structural tension charting at our company, we have encouraged every employee to work on at least one personal goal he or she wants to create. We usually pick one that has at least two criteria:

1. Something the person wants that is a bit of a challenge; and
2. Something that has a due date of two to six months.

The idea is that when people learn to create important personal goals within that type of time frame, they begin to experience their own ability to create what they want in their lives. They have their organizational experience with structural tension charting, but they also have created something for themselves, too. This helps their organizational work, and we like being able to help them in their lives.

A Little Lesson in Learning

We do not learn the same lesson over and over. Learning is a cumulative process, and past learning becomes the foundation of new learning. For this reason, using structural tension, people increase their effectiveness over time and experience.

The following illustration shows how learning happens within the context of structural tension.

Once we have established our goal in relationship to our current reality, we take an action:

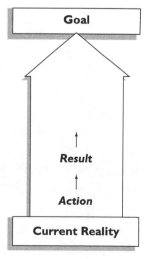

There is a consequence to the action, and therefore, it leads to some form of outcome or result:

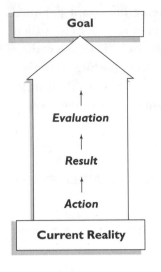

The result is evaluated: Did it help get us closer to the goal?

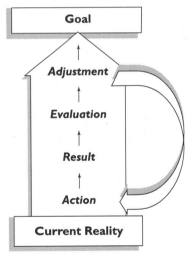

This then leads to an adjustment that feeds back into the system, and we take more effective actions in the future:

The cycle repeats itself until we achieve our goal. As the cycle repeats, a change occurs. With each repetition, we learn more. Our greater understanding and experience leads us to greater effectiveness. We are able to take better actions producing better results; make better evaluations, which leads to better adjustments; and so on. The progression is in refining and strengthening the process while increasing capacity.

beginning capability ⟶ **more capable** ⟶

action–result–evaluation–adjustment–action–result–evaluation–adjustment–action–result–evaluation–

more capable ⟶ **more capable** ⟶

adjustment–action–result–evaluation–adjustment–action–result–evaluation–adjustment–action–result–

⟶ **more capable** ⟶

evaluation–adjustment–action–result–evaluation–adjustment–action–result–evaluation–adjustment–action

An example of learning happened to Joe, a friend of mine. His boss was reluctant to develop a web site in-house, because he thought Joe incapable of making an effective one. But Joe convinced his boss to let him try, while the company was deciding on how to develop a "real" web site.

Joe's boss had very high standards, but he also had a "perfection thing"— very little tolerance for imperfection. The "perfection thing" made Joe's boss veto many things before they ever had a chance to develop and grow. He often paid subcontractors twice the going rate just to get a "professional product." He didn't realize that the subcontractors were going through the same stages of learning as his in-house staff, but, of course, they had the good sense never to show the work to their perfectionist client until the job was completely done.

But, this time, Joe got his chance. The first results were modest, and Joe's boss didn't like them. Joe's boss pointed Joe to various sites he liked. Joe studied them, and learned. Joe learned more and more, and the site became better and more effective. The hit rate to the site increased. Joe learned more about animation, web site graphics, load strategies, HTML code, and so on. Within three months, Joe had created a web site that many people rated as highest for production value and effectiveness. If Joe had been stopped the first time out because the web site wasn't perfect, he wouldn't have eventually created an effective one.

Learning is the key to developing professional competency. In the arts and in sports, people practice all the time. They take action, evaluate the results, make adjustments, and get better. They work within the context of structural tension, and, as it was for Joe, their path of least resistance is to move toward their goal, step by step, until they get there.

Adding Detail to the Master Chart

In this chapter, Structural Tension Charting consisted of a single chart, which shows the end result as contrasted with the current reality and the actions that are designed to accomplish the goal.

Charting may also consist of several related structural tension charts that develop the overall goal, first in a broad-brush level of description, and later in more and more details.

But regardless of the number of related charts, the starting point—the first structural tension chart—is always a Master Chart or a Project Chart. These are called *First Level Charts*.

The accomplishment of these goals on the Master Chart represents a major milestone in development and growth.

Adding layers of detail to the Master Chart or Project Chart — creating additional, related charts—is called *telescoping*, and that is discussed in the next chapter.

Quick Review

- Structural Tension Charting is a primary technique for establishing structural tension.

- In Structural Tension Charting, we first identify our overriding goals, and then those goals become the driving force for defining our current reality and creating our action plan to reach those goals.

- Each action step in a chart must have a due date and a person accountable for that step.

- Structural Tension Charting is very flexible. It can be used by senior management in a top-down planning process, by project teams, and even by individuals in their work or their personal life.

- The learning process involves a cycle of taking an action that produces a result, evaluating the result, making an adjustment, taking an action, and repeating the cycle until your goal is achieved.

- Structural tension facilitates the learning process, and thus increases a person's effectiveness over time.

Telescoping

Creating Organizational Counterpoint

On the master structural tension chart, each action step by definition describes a major action. But to accomplish each major action step, many other steps need to be taken. And all steps must be taken to create our goal.

How do we describe and organize these various activities? We could go crazy listing all the things we need to do because it can be quite overwhelming. So instead of driving ourselves to distraction, we will divide and think. We will use a technique called *telescoping*.

What Is Telescoping?

Telescoping is just as it sounds: something smaller is contained within something larger, and we can pull it out or leave it tucked in. Each action step on the master chart becomes the object of a new structural tension chart.

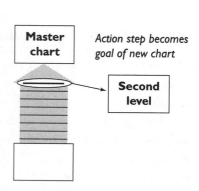

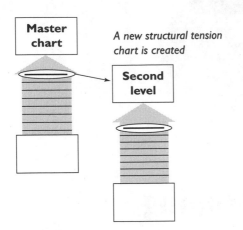

When the action step becomes the goal of the new telescoped chart, we next describe its current reality, action steps, due dates, and accountabilities.

Each action step on the Master Chart may have its own structural tension chart. Each new second level chart's may be further telescoped to third or fourth level charts, and so on This is where detail is developed.

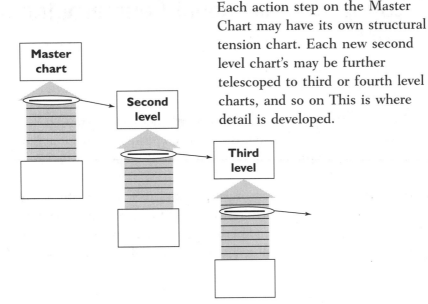

What Telescoping Produces

The wonderful thing about this process is that the division of mental labor doesn't fragment the organization; instead, the parts work together.

This process also provides everyone with an overview so no one gets lost in obsessive detail. People can see trees and know that they are part of a whole forest. This is a profound change of thinking, especially on the team level. When a group begins to see relationally, it gains insight into the organization as a structure and begins to have a feel for the principles of the path of least resistance. Team members come to realize that energy moves along the path of least resistance, structure determines the path, and to change the path, they need to change the structure. From this perception, they become wiser and more effective. They are less likely to react to situations, and instead, use the situations they find themselves in as current reality in their structural tension charts.

Controlled Autonomy

One of the beauties of telescoping is that it is highly organized without being micro-managed. People can use their own approach to get results, as long as it is consistent with the values and policies of the organization. Each manager has a degree of freedom to use his or her God-given talents and abilities.

For example, a pharmaceutical company's clinical research trial group began using Structural Tension Charting to manage its very complex project. The group was conducting a clinical study designed to test an anti-viral drug and, if it were found safe, bring it through the FDA regulatory process.

Starting with the goal of receiving FDA approval—the desired state—they developed the original structural tension chart. Achieving this goal required a structural tension chart with twenty-three major action steps. Each step was then in turn telescoped into a structural tension chart. Finally, these twenty-three charts were telescoped into 144 charts. These charts represented the major elements of the project.

The senior manager of the group worked with her team by managing the master plan—the original structural tension chart. She also used her technical expertise to guide the process as difficulties and challenges arose, and to stay current with the very latest science concerning the disease related to their drug. The accountability for each of the other charts was assigned to a person in one of the clinical teams, and two particular managers were assigned the task of coordinating the workflow.

These two managers set up what they called the *war room*—a room in which they could hang all of the structural tension charts around the walls. Anyone visiting that room could see the current state of the project in any of its phases.

One of the two managers used traditional project management techniques in conjunction with the structural tension charts, working with members of the group to make sure that the trials were being carried out on time and within the correct protocol. Using each team's structural tension charts, the managers could easily track actions and update current reality as it changed. New steps were added as needed, and adjustments were continually made to support the time lines the group had created.

The other manager coordinated the flow and the relationships among the various charts so that, as the situation changed, an early warning system could alert the rest of the key players and they could re-plan as needed.

This was a good system: leadership management for the major structural tension chart, project management for the teamwork, and an overall manager who was coordinating and integrating the entire effort. Pharmaceutical development is especially relational because every part is inextricably tied to the other parts. Information must be tracked and recorded precisely and the protocol must be adhered to with great discipline and rigor. Structural Tension Charting was particularly well suited to the demands of such a regimen.

The clinical research trial group got its FDA approval in an accelerated time frame, and the drug now makes over $600 million a year for the company, while helping its target patient group.

Seeing the Whole Picture

Gary Ralston, a structural consultant and partner of Ralston Consulting, reports on his use of structural tension charting:

> One of our clients boiled a complex, urgent development project down to a master chart and fifteen sub-charts. By tacking them up on a wall and studying them all at once, she was able to discern key relationships between sub-tasks that had previously been hidden from view. She called in one of her colleagues, the person managing the technology developments of the project and, standing in front of the charts, reworked the approach they were taking. This change would never have happened if they were not able to see the entire project as parts

related to the whole, something that would have been unlikely without the structural tension charting process. This insight led to design changes that shortened the development cycle, which was vital, given the company's deadlines.

Focusing the Work of Teams

Even teams operating within a large organization can use structural tension charting to accomplish projects more effectively and efficiently. Barry Sagotsky, an in-house training manager and structural consultant for Schering-Plough Pharmaceuticals, describes his use of structural tension charting with eighteen people from a health care systems group:

> They had to put together a white paper about whether or not to get into a particular business. Typically white papers in this organization take months to complete. We built the overall strategy for building a business at a certain volume over a five-year period—a master structural tension chart and thirteen telescoped elements, each with their own structural tension charts.
>
> It was complete enough in the two days that we took to do the planning, that about 90 percent of the paper was completed. In two days! And this was a group that included three members who opened up their introduction of themselves by saying, "I don't think we can do this with this group, and I object to being here." At the end, the entire group had focused on making all thirteen steps in the structural tension charts happen.

Composing the Organization

This process of structural tension charting and telescoping is very much like a compositional process in music. We are organizing multiple events so that they work together and support each other.

Telescoping reinforces structural tension as the dominant structure within an organization. It also helps an organization become a unified whole like a well-formed piece of music. As La France's George Barrar reported:

> These days we see interconnectedness throughout the business—how the different departments impact each other as part of our master design. We took our business strategy and then made strategic plans for each particular business unit across the

corporation. When we put all the structural tension charts on the wall, it was really pretty obvious what the priorities were—where we needed to build up capacity, and where we needed to shift our focus, and where we didn't need to do what we thought we needed to do. It was pretty easy to make important decisions about direction and strategy, and now the organization is tremendously focused, and everything supports everything else.

Structural Tension Charting in a Manufacturing Company

In a conference on the structural approach in organizations, Gordon Baker,* CEO for a mid-sized manufacturing company, and Rick Coulton, director of human resources, gave the following report about using a structural approach in their organization, a company with two divisions: the manufacture of high tech equipment that tests the hardness of various materials, and the manufacture and distribution of a plastic tubing.

> Rick: In the past we had strategic business plans. Like most businesses do.
> Gordon: Yeah, short-term, unconnected plans. More localized plans. Like most other businesses. We started building our strategic plan with structural tension charts and, after we had set them up, we had subsequent meetings to condense and rework them. We could really see the tension building. People were moving toward something that was meaningful to our business. Now we have comprehensive plans where everything fits together within the whole business.
>
> Rick: We ended up with a really comprehensive business and management strategy. The two pivotal points of our business strategy translated into 22 major action steps.
>
> Gordon: The beauty of this kind of well-designed structure is that nothing is arbitrary and people know that it's relevant—

---

*Since this conference, Gordon Baker has left his company to become a structural consultant for other companies.

versus, "We're doing a bunch of stuff and we don't know why we're doing it." Now, everything is driven by two key business strategies, from which we branched off management strategies.

Subsequently, we ended up with local strategies coming off each one of those management strategies, which were really down at the level of getting the work done. So right now we're managing, I believe it's somewhere in the range of 40 structural tension charts that are linked back to these other management strategies, that are linked back to our business strategies. So everything is linked to everything else. No matter what you're working on, you know why you're doing it, all the way back up to our major business strategies.

Rick: There's a real clarity within the company now, because you're either working on one of two things: You're either doing core business strategy or you're working on growth strategy. Where before, with all the trainings, it was all "fluffy." You wondered, "What am I getting out of this?"

Gordon: Core business is our day-to-day operations— processing orders, making stuff, getting it out. But people now really understand the relationship between the core business and our growth strategy.

Rick: And people are really working well together.

Gordon: Cooperation's much better . . .

Rick: And, where before, when we tried to get something done, people felt "Well, hey, I've got other stuff I gotta work on." And you could never get things done right away. But now, people see what's needed and why, and they help get the job done.

Gordon: It's also easier to set up a hierarchy of what's to be worked on. However, we do have some bottlenecks—some limited resources in a given area. It's far easier to see what we need overall, and how we're going to (on a hierarchical basis) come up with decisions on what to work on first and what we can temporarily set aside.

Rick: Before, when we would change direction, it was "Ah, cripes, here we go again." But the other benefit is that now they know what's going on. "OK, if we need to move up this action step then, all right, let's put this other action step back here." And it's energetic, because everybody's aware of what we're trying to accomplish. They can see it. It's tangible.

Gordon: Exactly. They see why something's being set aside. Before, they didn't. Now, because the structure's in place, everyone knows exactly where and why changes fit in.

Rick: And we make decisions faster. We just had a case where we wanted to make a major decision about adding capacity.

Gordon: Right.

Rick: Now, normally, we would have gotten as far as saying, "We know we gotta do something here," but somehow it would never have gotten done. Now, within ten minutes, we made a decision. Everybody was in agreement with it, and we looked at each other thinking "Who are these people?" Twelve months ago that decision probably wouldn't have been made. We would have backed down. But now, when it was first brought up—"Hey, I think we want to move this item up on our list"— we were able to say "Here's what's involved with this. So we're going to have to take a piece of this out. OK, move it up."

Gordon: It would have taken us an hour and a half to discuss it and nothing would have been decided; it would probably have been put off for another meeting. Actually, meetings are almost nonexistent now. In fact, we just huddle at the end of the week. Our management groups stand around structural tension charts and, basically, report in on what we're doing. If we've got to change some dates or change some priorities, at that time we decide what we're going to do, and we understand why we're going to do it.

Rick: Takes about a half hour.

Gordon: A half hour. That's another big change. Before, the management meetings went nowhere and they were taking up a lot of time. We were holding meetings every week whether we needed them or not. Sometimes the meetings were dragging into two and three hours, with not really much being accomplished. We were killing our own productivity by spending time in meaningless meetings. Now, I think our organization has more of the characteristics of an organization that is learning. We are definitely able to work more effectively as a team. I mean, you can actually see people working interdependently. Now they understand their relationship to one another—that they are interdependent. Everyone can see how it's working, why it's working. So by having—and working with—the structural tension charts, they feel better about what they are doing. They're proud of their accomplishments. Last year we were only at 17% growth, but we're on our target for a 25% increase this year.

The Tactical Approach

As people begin to work out the actions involved in their level 2 and further telescoped charts, they begin to need to move beyond what could seem like a "to do" list, and to a real understanding of actual tactics that are involved with supporting the strategy.

A strategy describes the entire concept of engagement (more in Chapter 11). Tactics are like little strategies, or the specific approach that people take in the local domain that supports the goals that the strategy demands.

We are better off when we have a general notion of what we are doing, rather than simply a list of actions we need to complete.

To illustrate this point, let's look at a second-level structural tension chart that deals with optimizing the manufacturing capacity of a company that develops and produces chemical products.

Optimize Production

- Revamp cooling and heating system to handle increased capacity
- Upgrade key equipment
- Divide plant into 3 areas to facilitate staggered shutdowns
- Create efficient 12-hour/7-day work week
- Expand chiller capacity. Define/evaluate plantwide system
- Cooling water system capacity and piping distribution systems–upgrade
- 16-hour/7-day analytical coverage
- SOPs for routine operations
- Increase bulk storage
- Formalize operator training program
- Define desired inventory levels of certain products
- Have a capacity measurement task force
- Develop a manpower plan
- Capacity evaluation on current equipment
- Evaluate on-site alternative for expansion
- Enforce firmer schedules
- Coordinate training and maintenance downtime
- Source second vendors for key raw materials
- Control the flow of production and focus attention on bottlenecks

50% on-time delivery, 80–85% on-time renegotiated delivery dates. 3–4 month backlog. No capacity measuring systems. Arbitrary standards of yield, raw materials, etc. We have structure but do not have a method to verify practicality of standards. 7-day work week in place, but only 75% staffed. Several bottlenecks.

Grouping by Type of Action

The above Structural Tension Chart has 19 action steps, all of which were themselves telescoped, creating an enormous amount of detail. How can the managers who are accountable for these action steps understand how they all fit together? This is an important question because it is easy to get lost in the details and think in terms of "to dos" only, and lose the overall shape and relationship among the parts.

One step we can use is to group actions by the type of activity it is. There are several ways we can look at the above list. Here is an easy and simple method:

- Systems

- Equipment

- Personnel

- Training

- Physical organization and storage

- Scheduling

Every action step falls into one of these categories, and that helps us understand the types of general activities we are using to optimize production capacity. This is useful to know, because it gives us a quick understanding of what we are doing to optimize the plant. When people get a little lost or overwhelmed, they can remember the function of the steps they are taking, and this can produce clarity.

Understanding the Tactic

While it is useful and good to know the types of actions we are taking, an even more useful technique is to understand the overall tactical concept of the approach we are taking. Often, I ask managers to think of time in terms of phases. Each phase represents a different point in time, a different type of activity, a different relationship among the various parts, and a building sense of momentum. The test of a good strategy or tactic is that each step builds on the previous steps. By taking each step, it becomes easier to take the subsequent steps.

Phase 1 is usually the beginning in which we find easy-to-take actions. We want to create early success to get us into the swing of our tactic, and so we can create some good germinational energy to help propel our approach. Phase 2 is usually how we integrate our early successes and build upon them. Phase 3 creates our longer term involvement and creates a solid foundation upon which we can develop our more complex aspects of our tactic. For some tactics there may be a phase 4 or even 5, each one developing a more involved and complex aspect of the approach.

Our example structural tension chart is a phased look at a possible tactic. Since the plant is currently running in the beginning of our tactic, we must treat phase 1 with an understanding that we are engaged in a continuing activity that needs to be developed even as it is maintained. Phase 1 needs to include the idea of operating better with what we've got. Once we do that, we are able to move into what could be phase 2; creating new systems and procedures. In phase 2, we might be adding more storage and equipment, as well as increasing our personnel numbers. In phase 3, we expand our overall capacity, perhaps adding a new plant.

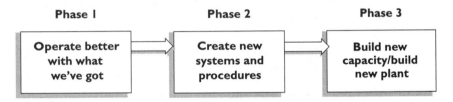

To better describe our overall tactic, let's describe it as if we were appointed head of a college basketball team in the middle of a season. Since we came in mid-season, we would have games to play, and we must make the most of the team we have and the resources we have available to us. This would be our phase 1. The next phase might be to rethink our entire approach to our game. We might hire a new coach, and spend our summer practicing. Phase 3 might represent our recruitment of highly talented players and better training systems. We would begin to go after conference titles and win most of our games.

This analogy is helpful in thinking about our general approach to accomplishing our goal of optimizing our plant. It is easy to understand, it reflects the action steps we have on our structural tension chart, and it is easy for everyone to understand and be able to support. The details become part of the tactic, rather than a bunch of "to dos" that aren't immediately understandable.

Once you create your action steps within your structural tension charts, translate them into classifications and tactical phases, and you and your team will have a better understanding of your approach to achieving your goals.

Control

Structural Tension Charting helps every manager have real control. But let's talk for a moment about the confusing subject of control, a very complex topic within management circles. As managers, we need control, and yet we do not want to act in controlling ways. How can we be effective without being a pain to everyone?

A pattern that we see is that of managers who rightly want to have control of their work, but don't know how to accomplish it. So first they try to take a "hands-off" approach. But, after a while, things start to go wrong. Deadlines are missed, bad decisions are made, and the project gets out of control. The manager tries to save the day by coming in, all guns blazing, and takes full control of the entire project. Nobody works well under a tyrant, or a micro-manager. The micro-management runs amok and people react. After some early gain from the manager's dramatic intervention, the people begin to underperform, and the manager becomes overwhelmed with all the details he or she is trying to handle. The manager realizes that this is more than one person can deal with and backs off. But, backing off just puts the manager back in the same condition that led to being controlling. In this pattern, too little is followed by too much is followed by too little.

Tiger Woods has control. Al Pacino has control. Martina Hingus has control. Michael Jordan has control. Mariah Carey has control. Steven Spielberg has control. Great race drivers, great architects, and great surgeons have control. Without control, they would not be able to do their jobs. To do your job, you need control. But when we talk about control, there can be profound misunderstanding about what it is. Don't get nervous. We are not talking about you becoming a willful jerk so you can better manipulate people to succumb to your wishes. People who are excessively controlling act that way because they do *not* have control, not because they have it. With the right leadership qualities and structural support, people will want to join with you. They will want to contribute their talents and energy to accomplish the common goal. And Structural Tension Charting gives you control without having to resort to being Dr. Fu Man Chu or a boss worthy of a Dilbert cartoon. Everyone can deal with one another professionally and objectively as they can see the logic of the approach they are taking to achieve their goals. They can see the logic as the action steps are telescoped into other charts showing the right level of detail as the process reaches other levels of development.

Real Results™ Manager (RRM): The Software

How many levels can we telescope? It depends on the organization and the way the organization is using structural tension charting. Many mid-size companies use structural tension charting throughout the organization. In a top-down approach, the senior people manage the master level chart, and some 2nd or 3rd level charts. The charts are telescoped down four or five levels. This produces hundreds and even thousands of charts. This can produce a type of orchestral compositional kind of control, or get out of hand. How can so much information be coordinated so that it is useful rather than overwhelming?

The answer is software. The actual software product that can generate and coordinate all of this information easily and intuitively is called Real Results™ Manager (RRM). It is software that I initially designed for my clients to automate the process that originally was done on flipcharts. This process can be done without software, but, personally, I would never do it without RRM anymore than I would try to write a book without using a word processor, now that they are available.

How the Software Works

RRM is a network based multi-user database type of software. The information sits in a database that the users have access to through their terminals. Structural tension charts are organized in levels from the master chart to 2nd, 3rd, 4th levels, and so on. Users open up the program and can locate the charts they need to work on. A manager can open the program and see how his or her direct reports are doing: are they on time, has current reality changed, are we on track, do they need any support? The people who have been assigned various action steps to manage can telescope up and see the logic that drives what they are doing. Information can get to the right people at the right time so decisions can be made more quickly and effectively.

The software automates a process that I have used for years with my clients mechanically. You can use structural tension charting without having to get the software. It is a convenience of course. But the bigger the organization or the bigger the user group coordinating their efforts though structural tension charting, the more the automation is essential. When a company gets to the point of three or four thousand charts, as some of our client companies have, it's hard to imagine coordinating all of that information and activity without the software.*

Using Structural Tension Charting in a School System

Sherry Sparks, a structural consultant who specializes in education, has been using a structural approach with many of her client organizations for the past year. One example is the Allen Park School System in Michigan. Before the approach was used, there were typical organizational problems at Allen Park. They had trouble keeping in mind long-range results and the big picture when they planned. Implementation was difficult. Individual schools in the system wanted to align their action plans with the district's goals, but found themselves consumed by immediate events, too much detail, and "administrivia." From time to time, they would glimpse the big picture they wanted, but they weren't able to use this information in any practical way.

---

*For a free demonstration copy of Real Results™ Manager, call 1-800-848-9700 or 1-802-348-7176.

Their decisions appeared unconnected to their long-range goals. Lack of specificity led to confusion, cynicism, and empty compliance. This behavior was against the nature of the caring, competent professionals in the Allen Park system. Individuals, small groups, or committees made decisions that seemed appropriate given immediate circumstances but were counterproductive in the long run to achieving their goals.

People couldn't seem to get the information they needed. People became mistrustful and began to assume the worst. One process after another was adopted, with people putting in long hours, feeling overwhelmed, but seeing little improvement. People left, but the new people began to act like the people they replaced in no time at all. Such is the way of the path of least resistance—the structure of the organization, more than the good intentions of the good people involved, drove them where they didn't want to be.

The group began the process of creating structural tension, and then Structural Tension Charting, using the RRM software. From looking at their goals and reality, the group learned the following things:

- The school district tried to be everything to everyone.

- School district employees worked incredibly hard, but results, in terms of student performance or success later in life, were undetermined.

- Their "customers" went beyond their community: they included local, state, and national legislators (who funded and evaluated the system); higher education (who could accept or reject their students); and their student's future employers.

- Stating their values and goals was important, because their employees and residents were unable to determine whether their values and goals matched.

- Their wants and values were very similar to those of their students and community.

- Their decisions did not consistently match their values.

- The decisions did not help students clarify their values and goals.

- Their employees and community wanted timely information about the school district.

- Their school district's funding could be greatly increased by thinking entrepreneurily. Many existing programs could be expanded and utilize, in mutually beneficial ways, the knowledge, skills and exceptional talents of their employees.

As we can imagine, this was a gutsy group of people who could look at themselves with such objectivity. They created a series of structural tension charts and put them into practice. The results were dramatic. Here's what Sherry reported:

> Our client's results and values are now clear to everyone, the school district is making better use of its time, facilities, and resources. They have greater alignment of everyone affecting our students. They can focus what ever processes they choose to use directly to the results they want to create. They have moved from studying and following current educational trends, to thinking originally and independently. They use best practices when it makes sense, and not if it doesn't, and they are becoming increasingly creative. They have gone from a "putting out the fires" mindset to creating long term goals for their students.
>
> The feeling has changed, and people are now really involved in a new way. Their decisions are better. They are less reactive. They are accomplishing their goals.
>
> And the approach is spreading. This year, the whole system will use Structural Tension Charting and use the RRM software as a visual means of viewing and tracking what's going on in the school district. Soon, families and community can access our structural tension charts from their homes and workplace to stay in touch with how we're doing.

Divide and Think

When we create the master structural tension chart and then develop the details through telescoping, we use a critical thought process that could be called *divide and think*.

We think about, first, the desired outcomes; second, our current situation; third, our general approach to moving from our current situation to our desired one; and fourth, the breaking down of the general steps into more details about implementation.

This is otherwise often very hard for people to accomplish in the hustle and bustle of organizational life. A common mistake that many people make is to fuse everything together into a big mish-mash. If you analyze many business and management meetings, you hear something like this:

Okay, what's the agenda?

We need to get a decision about the subcontractor.

I thought we hired them.

Who?

Bogen and Co.

We said we weren't going to use them anymore.

Who said that?

I thought . . .

No, that was . . .

Can't we make a decision around here?

I remember when I worked for International . . .

You and your International experience. Why did you ever leave?

He had to.

I did not.

Well, let's stay on course.

Right, so what are we talking about?

We need to hire Bogen.

Why?

Because we said we would.

No we didn't. We said we think about a subcontractor.

We need that order out.

We can handle it ourselves.

How? They're backed up for weeks down at the plant.

I talked to Fred.

Fred? What does Fred know?

I don't think you should have talked to Fred.

Why not?

Because he's a nice guy. He'll try to get our order though, and screw up everything else.

We need a better system at the plant.

We need another plant.

We can't afford that.

Who says?

The boss.

Yeah, it's not his problem. He just lays it on us, and we have to figure out how we can pull rabbits out of a hat without any budget.

True.

Yeah.

Why can't we get the funds we need? It's stupid.

They spent it on that corporate showpiece.

Who was the architect?

Oh, that weird guy. The one with the earring.

Three earrings.

Watch it, my son wears an earring, and he's a good kid.

It's just style. You know, next they'll be piercing their elbows.

They already do.

They do?

Can we get back on the subject?

Who does?

Well . . .

Can we please . . .

I think that you should call Bogen and . . .

How about TTF?

They always let us down.

We only used them once.

Yeah, but, it was important. The client was really mad.

We should never have taken the order.

Those sales guys, they don't care.

Yeah.

In conversations like this, people are more likely to free-associate than use a disciplined thought process. Our thought process is better served by using the *divide and think* method in which we focus on only one type of topic area at a time.

Whenever you or your team is in the thick of it, you can focus the discussion by asking the following questions that help locate the important areas we need to be aware of, and then see them in relationship to each other:

Reminders to help keep focus

- What is the end result we want?
- What is current reality—*now*?
- What steps do we need to take to get to our end result?
- Are our actions working?
- What are we learning?
  —Is there another approach that might be better?
  —How do we know if we are on track?

It's amazing how the three or four minutes it takes to ask and answer these questions can transform everyone's experience. From an experience of disorder, people move to order.

Quick Review

- Telescoping is a technique for adding progressive levels of detail to a Structural Tension Chart.

- This detail is added in a deliberate and organized manner that facilitates planning.

- In telescoping, for each action step in the Master Structural Tension Chart, we can create an individual structural tension chart. Then we can create an additional chart for each step in the second chart, and so on, as needed.

- Telescoping helps create structural tension by bringing a unity to the organization, because each action, no matter how minor, can be traced back to the organization's major goals and its current realities.

- Charting and telescoping can be done either manually or with software.

- A thought process that is helpful in creating structural tension charts is called *divide and think*.

- When you are in the "thick of it," you can first, identify your desired outcome; second, determine current reality; and third, create an action plan to move you from current reality to your desired outcome. This will help focus you and your team.

CHAPTER
.5

Checklists

Refining the Chart

When you develop structural tension charts, your first draft will likely be followed by a second draft and perhaps a third, as you refine your goals, descriptions of current reality, and action steps. To help you in this process, I have put some basic principles about structural tension charting in the form of checklists.

There are two ways to use this chapter. One is as a quick read to survey the points. The other is as a reference. When you have written a structural tension chart and you are ready to refine it, have your structural tension chart out, and go through each of the checklists. This will help you aim your work with more focus.

Checklist for Goals

If your chart is a master chart, your end result will describe overall outcomes, your final destination—where you want to arrive and what you want to create.

As you think about your end results, you can check them against the following checklist.

1. Is this the result we want to create? Form a mental picture of the results you described.

If the answer is yes, you have described what you want. By going through the rest of this checklist, you will be able to refine your goals, and this will make it easier to organize around them.

If the answer is no, then there is more work to do. Continue to describe the result you truly want to create. But don't get fooled into thinking that more and more details give you more and more information. The level of description you need for the result on the Master Chart level should be broad rather than overly detailed, clear rather than vague, the overview rather than the minute.

2. Did you quantify the goal wherever you could?

Whenever you can, assign actual numbers to your goals. It is easier to organize your actions when you know that the result is $285 million, rather than "high revenues." Aim your sights clearly and directly. To do this, you will need to make real decisions about what you want to create.

Besides money, there are other factors that may be in your Master Chart end result that are better off quantified. For example, if you have a profit goal, put a number on it: 20% profit margin, for example. Other examples of quantifying are 16 new office locations, or 28 new major accounts and 80 minor ones.

Each time you put a number on an element that can be quantified, you define that element more clearly. It also gives you more clarity when you define current reality. So get into the habit of assigning the actual numbers, and you will develop more precision and power in your ability to produce result!

3. Did you translate comparative terms into their actual goals?

Comparative terms—such as *more, better, less,* or *increased*—have meaning only when seen in relationship to something else. "Better communication," for example, doesn't quite tell us what we want, because if communication is very bad, better communication may still be inadequate. And inadequate communication probably is not what you want to create!

Rather than use comparative terms, describe the result you actually want; in this case, good communication.

Here are some more examples of this principle:

Rather than write *More product development*, write *Seven new product releases per year.*

Rather than write *Increased sales*, write $55 *million in sales from the WX-T12.*

Rather than write *Better management decisions*, write as a goal: *We continually make the right decisions at the right time.*

4. Are you creating results or just solving problems?

As Chapter 7 will discuss, problem solving is taking action to have something go away: the problem. Creating results is taking action to have something come into being: the full achievement of your goals. If you write your end results from a problem solving point of view, you only eliminate or avoid something, rather than create and build something. So, here is a major secret: Describe what you want to create rather than what you want to eliminate.

Here are some examples of this principle:

Rather than write *Overcome our company's lack of marketing ability*, write *Great marketing that tells our clients our story and creates conditions in which they want to buy our products.*

Rather than write *Fix our capacity strain*, write *Adequate (or optimal) workload/capacity relationship.*

Rather than write *Get rid of excessive overtime*, write *Well-planned and executed work schedule.*

5. Do your goals describe an actual result or only a process for achieving that result?

Process tells us the HOW—how do we accomplish our goals. *End results* tell us the WHAT—what do we want to accomplish? Process always serves an end result; that is its purpose. In the Master Chart, the end result should describe outcomes rather than processes—the WHAT rather than the HOW.

Here are some examples of this principle:

Rather than write *Create a task force for IT* (Information Technology), write *We have an IT system that is robust and can grow over time as our needs grow.*

Rather than write *Get support for the business strategy from all our key players*, write *Business strategy is in place and generating dynamic growth.*

Rather than write *Develop an integrated R&D and production system*, write *R&D and production are working as an integrated whole and reinforcing each other.*

6. Are your goals specific or vague?

If your end result is specific rather than vague, you can more easily organize around it. As we said in the beginning of this checklist, if an item on your list can be quantified, do so. When items are not so easily quantified, aim for the greatest degree of specificity you can.

Here are some examples of this principle:

Rather than write *Happy customers*, write *Our customers are satisfied with our services, and we enjoy a return rate of 85% on repeated sales.*

Rather than write *Great products!*, write *Our products are rated highest on our customer survey reports.*

Rather than write *We innovate*, write *Three new technologies created and used in our products.*

Because defining your goals is the driving force in Structural Tension Charting, spend time to make sure that the checklist principles above have been met.

Checklist for Current Reality

Now that you have determined the major goals in your Master Chart, it's time to describe current reality. Those goals tell us about your final destination, while describing current reality tells us your starting point on that journey.

1. Did you use your goals as a reference point in describing current reality?

For example:

If your goal is $48 *million in annual sales*, describe your current sales in current reality as $31 *million in sales*.

If your goal is *100% on-time delivery*, describe your current percentage of on-time delivery as *89% on-time delivery*

For every goal in your Structural Tension Chart, make sure the current situation for that goal is described in the current reality box.

2. Have you described the relevant picture?

3. Have you included the whole picture?

For example, your goal may be to put in a new quality program. In the current reality box you could say, *Don't have one*. While that would be true, it might be expressed more completely:

We don't have a formal quality system, although people see the need for more quality in our products. Customer surveys report dissatisfaction with our current quality. We have a training specialist in-house that has had some experience with quality, and the management team is overworked and a bit resistant to any change right now.

Notice that the second description gives us more of a picture of our starting point.

4. Translate assumptions and editorials into objective news reports.

Look out for assumptions that you may have built into current reality. Instead of assumptions, describe reality as objectively as you can.

For example, you might describe current reality as follows:

We don't have any business trying to go after business outside of our niche market.

This description gives us the editorial, not the news. For current reality, we want just the facts. When we have a more objective view of current reality, we are more able to design effective actions that can help us create the results we want.

With this in mind, we can translate the editorialized version of current reality to the following:

We have tried to do business outside of our market, but we got only a small return on our investment. We didn't know how to do it.

Now we can shorten this description to:

We currently do not know how to do business outside of our market.

5. Have you told the story without exaggeration?

Avoid exaggerations that describe reality either better than it really is, or worse than it is.

Instead of saying, *We have the worst record on safety*, say *We had 9 near misses and 1 minor accident this past year.*

6. Did you state what reality is, or just how it got to be that way?

You could write:

We bought a new kettle for the plant, and by the time we installed it, the sales guys had drummed up so many new orders that we couldn't keep up. So we had to put on a new shift, but they were untrained and we didn't make a lot of headway, but our costs went up. The customers weren't getting their orders when we promised, and everyone was mad at us and blaming us, but it was really the fault of the sales guys overpromising again.

This, however, is talking about the journey to where you now are, not where you are. So instead, write:

Our capacity is strained, more orders than we can handle. Sales and manufacturing are not coordinated. New people have taken more time than we thought to come up to speed. Our costs went up when we added the new shift.

7. Have you included all of the facts you need?

You may need to include other facts to fill in the picture of current reality. Here are some areas you may need to describe:

Current sales

Current market trends

Current market share

Current competition

Current financial conditions

Current product quality

Current distribution systems

Current capacity and available resources

Current management strategies and attitudes

Current job market and hiring practices

Current systems

Current talent of members of the organization

Current core competencies

Current decision making processes

Current business approach

When describing current reality, remember to be complete, accurate, and objective.

Checklist for Action Steps

The following principles will help you refine your action plan.

1. **For each goal on the Master Chart, are there action steps involving each major aspect of the organization?**

For example, in the Master Chart, you may want one or two action steps in each of these areas:

- R&D
- Marketing/sales
- Manufacturing and production
- Quality
- Management
- Information systems

- Administration and infrastructure
- Product offering
- Customer relationships
- Shipping/transport/distribution
- Financial management
- New business development

In the Master Chart, you may use the terms *design* and *implement* to describe a sequence of actions that will be developed in detail as those steps are telescoped (Chapter 4). An action may read, *Design and implement a comprehensive marketing approach.* This is very broadly described, but it may be an important step in reaching the goal. Remember, details later.

2. Can you answer "Yes" to the Test Question: If we took these steps, would we achieve these results?

The answer to this question is either yes or no. If no, then continue to fill in more action steps until the answer is yes. If the answer is yes, you have completed writing your action steps.

3. Are your action steps accurate, brief, and concise?

Sometimes people tend to write too much detail in their descriptions of actions. One or two short sentences usually are better than many long sentences. Be brief. Picture the action step. This will help you target it.

4. Does every action step have a due date?

As discussed in Chapter 3, due dates add reality to your description of current reality. Due dates place each action into a time frame. If the action is accomplished by its due date, that action fits into the various actions that will create the goal.

5. Does every action step have an accountable person assigned to it?

One person should be held accountable for each action. Without someone assigned, the action is less likely to get done. A general rule of thumb is that only one person should be accountable for an action, rather than a group or a combination of individuals. This helps create focus and a valuable division of labor, as different managers have different accountabilities.

Using checklists may seem too mechanical, but they are intended to instill a discipline to your approach, much like the thought process, *divide and think*. Experiment with them and judge for yourself the great value they may provide.

Quick Review

- The checklist for Identifying Goals is:

   1. Is this the result you want?

   2. Did you quantify the results wherever you could?

   3. Did you translate comparative terms into their actual goals?

   4. Did you focus on getting what you want or only on eliminating problems?

   5. Did you describe the results you want or just the process for achieving those results?

   6. Did you describe your goals specifically, or are they vague?

- The Checklist for Determining Current Reality is:

   1. Have you looked at every goal in your Structural Tension Chart and described the current reality for that goal?

   2. Did you include what's relevant?

   3. Have you included the whole picture?

   4. Have you translated assumptions and editorials into objective news reports?

   5. Did you "tell it like it is" without exaggeration?

6. Did you state what reality is, rather than how it got to be that way?

7. Did you include all of the facts you need?

- The Checklist for Developing Action Steps is:

    1. Does the Master Chart include each major aspect of the organization and business?

    2 Can you answer "Yes" to the Test Question, "If we took these steps, does it look likely we would accomplish our goals?"

    3. Are your descriptions of the action steps accurate, brief, and concise?

    4. Does every action have a due date?

    5. Does every action step have a person accountable?

Take Away

If all you take away from this book is an understanding of how structural tension works and how you can use it, you will be greatly advantaged. However, you would not understand or be able to change what is going on when an oscillating structure is in play—where the organization advances, then regresses, then advances, and so on.

What causes organizations to oscillate? Why does the path of least resistance sometimes first lead to success, but then lead to reversals and even failure? These are important questions we will answer in Part 2 of this book.

THE PATH OF OSCILLATION

Structural Conflict
Why Organizations Oscillate

Most organizations have zillions of oscillating patterns that recycle regularly. Decision making can move from tightly centralized control, in which only the senior managers make all major decisions, to decentralized control, in which people from all over the organization are authorized to make major decisions. Once decentralized, though, the decision-making process can be recentralized again, and later, decentralized again. And on and on it goes.

Members of an organization may be encouraged to take "risks" and "independent action," then, later, asked to march in close step with senior leadership. Still later they are asked to act independently again.

The financial direction of the organization can move from cost-cutting to investment and then back to cost-cutting. The company as a whole can move from a "Let's be creative!" period, to "Let's benchmark and use conventional wisdom," but later, back to "Innovation builds our future!"

Organizations expand their capacity, then downsize, and then expand their capacity once again.

In these types of oscillating patterns, the organization squanders money, time, resources, intellectual capital, morale, reputation, and market share, not to mention that it seems to be suffering from manic-depression.

No one wants these oscillating patterns, so why do they exist? They exist because of a fundamental structure in which the path of least resistance makes it easiest to support first one course of action, strategy, or tactic, but then later its opposite. I call this structure *structural conflict*. When an organization chronically oscillates, structural conflict is in play. In this chapter, we'll explore structural conflicts and see why they produce oscillation.

What Causes Structural Conflicts

While a simple tension-resolution system causes structural tension, structural conflict is produced by a more complex structure: two competing tension-resolution systems based on two competing goals.

First, let's study how the structure works in a simple nonorganizational example.

Hunger is a tension that is caused by the difference between the body's desired amount of food and the actual amount of food it has. Hunger is a tension that is resolved by eating until the actual and the desired amounts of food are the same:

But if we are overweight (our actual weight is different from our desired weight), we form another tension-resolution system which is resolved by going on a diet:

As each system moves toward its own resolution, it competes with the conflicting system. First, the dominant, or most pronounced tension is hunger. In order to resolve that tension, we eat:

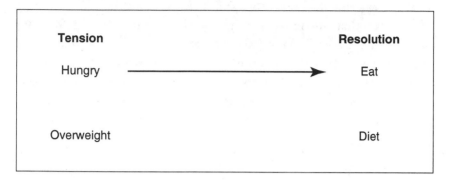

Once we have eaten, our hunger diminishes. But, unfortunately for most of us, our weight goes up. The amount we weigh is different from the amount we want to weigh. This difference then becomes the more pronounced tension:

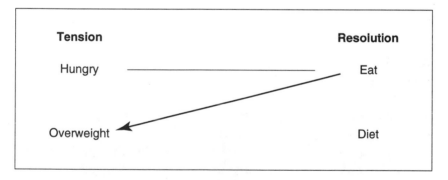

In order to resolve this tension, we may eat less, or skip meals:

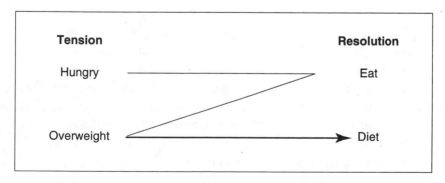

We may lose some pounds and we begin to feel better about our weight. But the body doesn't like this situation one bit and reacts to reduction of fat and protein by sending a starvation warning—"Eat! Eat! Eat!"—triggering the brain's appestat. (This is like a thermostat setting in the brain that concludes that the body isn't getting enough food. It's afraid that the body will not have enough fat stored in the winter, and the body will get cold.) Then the appestat does two things. It tells the body to eat—the hunger tension becomes the more pronounced one again, changing the path of least resistance—and the appestat tells the body to store more fat from less food. Depressing, isn't it?

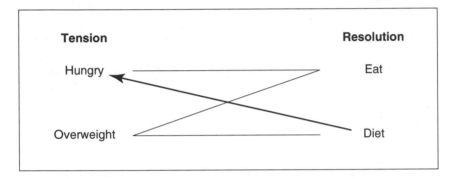

Tension	Resolution
Hungry	Eat
Overweight	Diet

A Shift in the Path of Least Resistance

This kind of movement between one tension-resolution system and its competing tension-resolution system is called a *shift of dominance*. A shift of dominance produces a predictable oscillating pattern, as the path of least resistance moves first to one type of action (eating, for example) to another (dieting). In our example, hunger leads to eating, which leads to weight gain, which leads to dieting, which leads to hunger, as the path of least resistance changes.

To anyone familiar with weight gain followed by dieting followed by more weight gain, it's easy to see that something weird is going on. What's not so easy to see is the structure causing the path of least resistance to change. People who experience this cycle may be afraid that they are to blame for being weak-willed or for lacking discipline. They do not realize that, within this structure, all the willpower in the world can't work. Every time they force themselves into a diet, the structure compensates for any movement, and eventually they have to fail. They are up against a structure that doesn't support them in creating what they want.

In structural conflicts, as one competing tension-resolution system moves toward resolution, the other tension-resolution system becomes dominant. Less tension in one leads to more tension in the other. This change produces a shift of dominance, but this shift is not permanent. Once the new higher tension begins to move toward its resolution, there is another shift of dominance back to the original, creating an oscillating pattern as shown in the accompanying illustration.

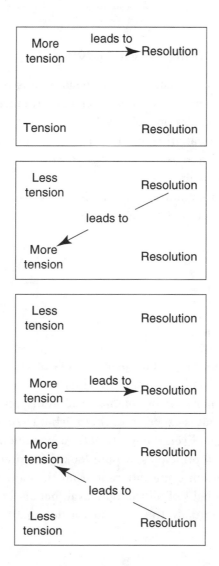

Here is the sixth inescapable law of organizational structure

> The SIXTH Law of Organizational Structure
>
> **When structural conflicts dominate an organization, oscillation will result.**

Oscillation within an Organization

Why do organizations oscillate? We can begin to answer this question by considering the sixth law of organizational structure, as it is illustrated in the following example.

The DDD Corporation wants to improve its performance, avoid stagnation, and capitalize on its potential. It puts in a big change program, and changes begin to happen all around the company. DDD's management team reorganizes systems, forms cross-discipline teams, adopts new evaluation methods, and moves people to new positions.

However, as the changes take place, people at DDD begin to feel a degree of instability and discontinuity. Their work becomes harder to accomplish as familiar lines of communication disappear. They begin to feel unsure of what is expected of them, what they need to do, and who is now in charge. Even though DDD's management clearly stated the new policies and principles, people look around and see that the actual conditions seem quite different from the new ideals that are being espoused. In light of all the upheaval, people begin to long for continuity, and eventually this becomes a dominant tension within DDD.

This tension is resolved by rejecting change. The people at DDD begin to bypass the new lines of authority and ignore the new policies. Support for the changes weakens as factions with their own agendas develop within DDD. The change effort is subtly undermined, and morale dips.

At this point in the cycle, DDD's management shifts away from its change effort, and the organization returns to business as usual. Everyone at DDD recognizes the change effort as a failure. But once they return to the old ways, they begin to feel growing pressure. Growth is limited, creativity restrained, and improvement stifled. After a time of living with stagnation, DDD's management begins to call for change again, particularly since they have become aware of a new management fad that has just become popular.

Over periods of years, the company cycles through several shifts between change and continuity. Each effort at change grows out of limitation and stagnation; each move back to the status quo comes from the discontinuity that change has brought.

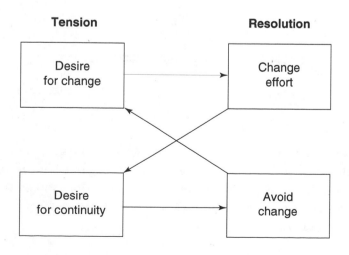

Many organizations are subject to this structure without under-standing the dynamics in play. Change is resisted, but so is stagnation. Continuity and change seem in a constant, unwinnable battle with each other. People often experience the frustration of neither losing nor gaining ground. Or perhaps every new change effort—for even the simplest advancements—requires mounting an enormous campaign. After a while, members of the organization may begin to wonder if change is worth the trouble.

What's Causing This Structural Oscillation?

Let's look more closely at the actual causes of these types of shifts. To demonstrate the dynamic nature of competing tension-resolution systems, imagine a rubber band tied around us as we attempt to resolve one of the tension-resolution systems: *change*.

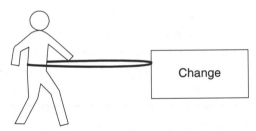

Now imagine another rubber band tied around us, but connected to our other desired state: *continuity*.

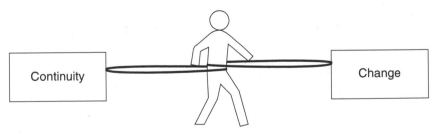

As we move toward the first of our goals—change—the tension-resolution system begins to resolve and things begin to change. As they do, what is happening to the other tension-resolution system, the rubber band connected to continuity? It is stretching, so tension in that system is increasing.

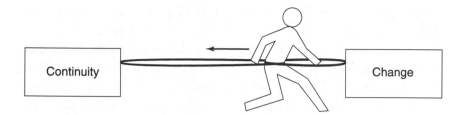

Now, where is it easier for us to move? Where does the path of least resistance lead? Obviously, away from the goal of change and toward the goal of continuity.

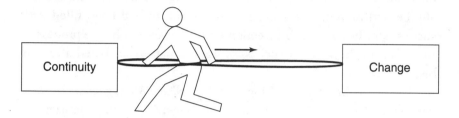

But as soon as the continuity rubber band begins to resolve, the change rubber band begins to stretch. Its tension is increasing. Where is it now easier for us to move? The path of least resistance leads us back toward change.

Oscillation between the theme of change and the theme of continuity repeats itself again and again. These shifts may take years to happen—so slowly that it is hard to observe a predictable pattern. This oscillating pattern can be disguised as other issues burst on the scene and demand attention, and events seem to rise out of the immediate situation. However, the real cause of these conditions will not be found in the issues, events or personnel, but in the structure that is inadequate for change, growth, or continuity.

Oscillation Undermines Change Efforts

Most attempts at change do not succeed. Is this because change, by its nature, is resisted? Common wisdom says change is hard. But is it hard when change is well motivated? I don't personally know anyone who would go back to a typewriter after using a word processor. Perhaps there is the rugged individualist, a self-styled Hemingway, somewhere who prefers to bang away on an old IBM electric or a mechanical Remington. But, if such a being exists, he or she would be the exception to the rule. (I suspect Hemingway would have been the first writer of his generation to switch to word processing if it had been available.)

Some change happens easily, overnight, and permanently. Organizational complexity notwithstanding, change can happen when the underlying structure supports it by creating a new advancing path of least resistance.

But when the dominant structure of an organization is structural conflict, and the path of least resistance is toward oscillation, then the most successful change program will lose its momentum and eventually be neutralized. The management literature had been filled with success stories about TQM, reengineering, or other change processes. But after all the years of success stories, a pattern of failed attempts began to surface.

Robert S. Kaufman, writing in MIT's *Sloan Management Review*, described the condition that many managers face in organizations dominated by structural oscillation:

> Your predicament as manager of a manufacturing revival is common: After years of educating yourself in the concepts of just-in-time and employee involvement, you launched an ambitious program in your company. After achieving dramatic productivity gains, you were convinced you were on the road to success. But the gains turned out to be only temporary, and now you're less optimistic. Employees are devoting less time to the program. Like failed initiatives of the past, it is being referred to with that terminal phrase, "just another program."
>
> You have tried all you can think of to revive the program, with little success. You are beginning to wonder whether you and your team have what it takes.

Since organizations must move along the path of least resistance, and their underlying structures determine the path of least resistance, the next logical question to ask is, "What does the structure want?" This question is important to answer if we are to understand why structural conflicts work the way they do.

What the Structure Wants

The situation is this:

- Two tension-resolution systems are competing against each other.

- Each individual system has the goal of resolving that system's tension.

- But it is impossible to resolve both systems simultaneously, because whenever we move toward resolution in one system, tension in the other system intensifies, and the path of least resistance is to move to resolve this new tension.

- A repeated shift of dominance from one system to the other produces oscillation.

There is an imbalance. The structure wants to reduce the imbalance, to create a balance, or *equilibrium*, between the two tension-resolution systems—between the two goals.

When I say the structure "wants" balance, I do not mean to imply that the structure has a mind, a will of its own, a personality, or a vested interest in the outcome, anymore than gravity has. Structure, like gravity, is an impersonal fact of nature.

But while the structure wants equilibrium, we want something that will produce nonequilibrium. We may want change:

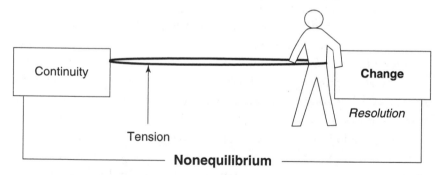

Or, we may want continuity:

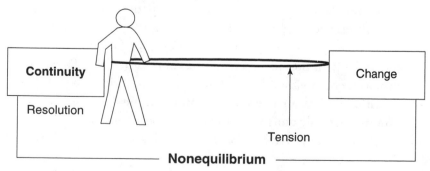

But the structure wants *balance* between the two competing tension-resolution systems, so that each tension equals the other:

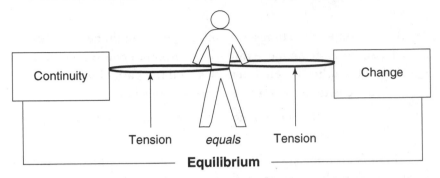

We must be aware of an important principle: *structure seeks equilibrium*. If a state of nonequilibrium exists, the structure will try to restore equilibrium, because its path of least resistance is toward equilibrium.

So, within the change-continuity structural conflict, anytime we move toward change, equilibrium is lost. If we move toward continuity, the equilibrium is also lost. Movement toward either side of the conflict sets up an imbalance.

Structural conflicts produce oscillating behaviors because any shift in dominance in one tension-resolution system leads to nonequilibrium. Once a state of nonequilibrium exists, the structure compensates by attempting to reestablish equilibrium, and the path of least resistance leads toward restoring balance between the competing tension-resolution systems.

As was said in Chapter 2, neither nonequilibrium nor equilibrium is necessarily good or bad. Some states of nonequilibrium manifest themselves as tensions that, like an archer's bow and arrow, can help us hit the targets at which we aim. Others, like pendulums, oscillate.

As human beings, we like to take sides whenever there is an argument or difference of opinion. But when we understand the structural dynamics in play, we are less likely to take sides between competing outcomes, be it on the side of change or continuity. This is because we know movement in either direction serves only to widen the magnitude of oscillation and create a tendency to move in the other direction.

But we certainly don't want to be stuck between change and continuity. And we don't have to be. Later in this book, we will explore how to deal with the structural conflicts in your organization. Don't worry. But, first, we need to study them and find out how and why they work the way they do.

So in the next two chapters, we will look, first, at an ineffective reaction to oscillation—the problem-solving approach to management—and then at the major structural conflicts you are likely to find in your organization.

Quick Review

Structural Conflict and Oscillation

- When two tension-resolution systems or two goals compete against each other, it produces a structural conflict.

- Oscillation operates as follows: As we move closer to one of our goals and farther from a second, competing goal, tension to move toward the second goal increases, and the path of least resistance moves us back toward the second goal. Thus, movement in one direction of a structural conflict will precipitate compensating movement in the other direction. Over time, oscillating behavior results.

- The sixth law of organizational structure is: When structural conflicts dominate an organization, an organizational oscillation will result.

- A structural conflict between two goals makes both goals difficult to accomplish, and the accomplishment will be reversed.

- Structure has the goal of establishing equilibrium between competing goals. When we move toward one goal, the structure automatically moves toward the other goal—in order to establish equilibrium—thus creating oscillation.

CHAPTER
7

The Problem with Problem Solving

Before we explore the most prevalent structural conflicts that organizations face, as we will do in Chapter 8, we must take a look at problem solving. Most people look at structural conflicts as problems to be solved. They are not, and so not only will problem solving not address an organization's oscillation, it can even cause oscillation.

Structural Conflicts Are Not Problems

Structural conflicts are not problems. They are simply structures that are inadequate to accomplish our ends. They are like rocking chairs: structures designed to oscillate. That's all they can do. If we found ourselves in a rocking chair but we wanted to travel downtown, we wouldn't attempt to "fix" our rocking chair by putting wheels on it or by installing a motor, steering wheel, and brakes. We would get out of our rocking chair and get into our car.

This is a good analogy for organizations. When we are confronted with inadequate structures, our temptation is to enter into a problem-solving mode, and try to fix what we think is wrong. We have been taught, when something is wrong, fix it. But fixing something ill-designed to begin with does little to help us achieve our aims. The seventh law of organizational structure tells us that organizations do not need fixing, they need to be redesigned.

> The SEVENTH Law of Organizational Structure
>
> **An inadequate organizational structure cannot be fixed. But you can move from an inadequate structure to a suitable structure.**

Fixing something means that we take what is there and repair it. *Redesigning* something means that we start from scratch and rethink the basic premises that guide us. It's better to rethink and redesign the organization than try to problem solve it. So why is problem solving popular?

The Lure of Problem Solving

Often, the first reaction managers have when they see a structural conflict is, "How do we solve it? How do we change it? How do we get rid of it? How do we get out of this!?" This is a natural reaction because we have been raised to be problem solvers. Particularly in the west, managers want to act whenever they see significant difficulties. Conflict, discrepancy, dilemmas and strife provoke us into a John Wayne, James Bond, Mel Gibson action mode.

But an obsessive focus on "What can we do?" leads us away from important fundamental questions: "How are we to understand the current situation?" or "What are the causes in play that create what we're living through?"

We tend to want to get rid of what we don't want before we understand what caused the situation. This is natural, and it takes discipline to not charge in with all guns blazing. But when we better understand why we have come to the situation that exists, we are often better able to take effective action on behalf of our goals, rather than ineffective action that may undermine our long-term aspirations.

Another reason managers love problem solving: It is a simple way to mobilize their people. People can easily understand the idea that something's wrong, and if we don't address it and address it fast, things are going to get worse. The immediate impact is that people can join together to generate action against a common enemy: the unwanted situation. If your house is burning down, you don't need to spend a lot of time contemplating a course of action. You have limited choices: Get everyone out, call the fire department, put it out yourself, or let it burn to the ground. After the fire, there is a built-in course of action: Call the insurance agent, and fight with the insurance company if it turns out not to be a good one.

Putting out a fire or dealing with the aftermath of a fire is different than building a house. Problem solving is vastly different from building, creating, generating something new. They lead to different results, and they lead to different structures. In fact, problem solving has a built-in structural tendency to oscillate. Let's see why.

How Problem Solving Causes Oscillation

In most traditional problem-solving techniques, we start by defining the problem, and then we generate an action plan designed to eliminate the problem. Our goal in this process is to get rid of the problem.

The more intense the problem, the more incentive we have to rid ourselves of it. But when we take the actions, we reduce the intensity of the problem. We feel better about the situation because we feel we are addressing it. However, once the problem is less intense, there is less motivation to take further actions.

Here's how the structure cycles through, forming an oscillating pattern:

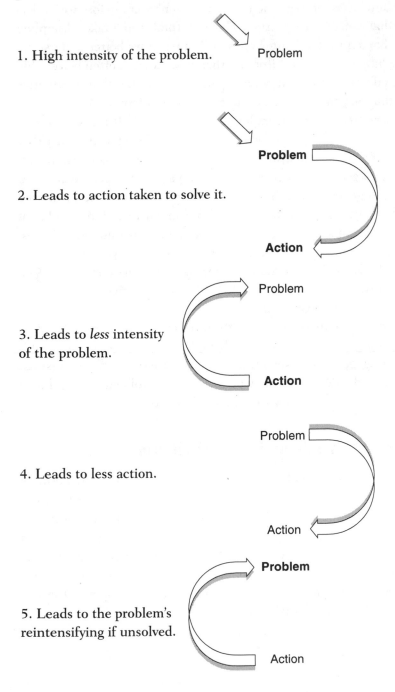

1. High intensity of the problem.

2. Leads to action taken to solve it.

3. Leads to *less* intensity of the problem.

4. Leads to less action.

5. Leads to the problem's reintensifying if unsolved.

This structure leads to a predictable pattern of oscillation: More intensity leads to more action, which reduces some of the intensity of the problem, which leads to less action.

At best, this strategy can work short-term to remove what we don't want. It cannot, however, help us create what we do want. Remember, taking out the garbage doesn't lead to a meal; eliminating and creating are not the same animal.

Let's now both summarize and expand on the reasons that problem solving causes oscillation, when problem solving is the major organizing principle within an organization.

First, actions will not be taken to move us toward our aspirations. Instead, people will react to the problems. They will be motivated by what they do not want, rather than by what they do want.

Second, as mentioned earlier, there is a difference between building demolition and architecture. One is taking action to have something go away, the other is taking action to have something come into being. This is the difference between problem solving and driving the organization by a vision of what we want to accomplish.

Third, organizational learning is limited to how to eliminate unwanted situations, not how to bring about desired situations. Therefore, learning would not provide the organization with added competency and capacity. And, were the problem-solving tactic truly successful, the problem would go away, leaving little application for learning in the future.

Fourth, motivation for action shifts from one problem to another as problems change in importance over time. In organizations with a problem-solving management style, different problems suddenly swing into focus at different times. With each new squeaky wheel, other squeaky wheels lose their fascination and importance. If you've taken action to get rid of a particular problem, the intensity of that problem may be significantly reduced; but even if the problem itself doesn't change, or if it gets worse, other problems will become more important and influential.

Fifth, a false impression of effectiveness is created within the organization, leading to questionable values (for example, that the time to act is when there is a crisis). During the heyday of problem-based management styles in the seventies and early eighties, many companies discovered that some of the best firefighters within their organizations also turned out to be pyromaniacs! The more rewards for dealing with crises, the greater the number of calamities. Some companies found that when they got rid of the firefighters, many of the fires went out.

Of course, organizations do have problems that need to be dealt with. Problem solving does have its place. But the better designed the business is, the less likely that problem solving is its primary orientation.

From TQM to Problem Solving to Oscillation

I love the quality movement. I particularly love Dr. W. Edward Deming's pioneering and revolutionary work. He was the real father of the quality movement and a true intellectual hero. Dr. Deming was the first to tell us that 94% of the difficulties businesses and organizations have are structural and systemic, and only 6% are caused by human folly. But many who have come after Dr. Deming translated his work into a problem-solving model, rather than understanding it as a reliable method for creating results. And by doing this, they have turned the quest for quality into a cause of oscillation.

Let's look at the structure of continual improvement when used as a simple problem-solving approach.

We begin with the current condition, then we analyze it, and finally we improve it.

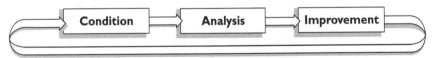

The driving, or generative, force within this process is found within the current condition. The analysis is designed to find imperfections within the current conditions. Improvements are designed to eliminate imperfections. Over time, fewer and fewer imperfections will be found as the improvements work.

However, as the situation improves (fewer defects), the driving force toward improvement is reduced—the process is moving toward inertia. Ironically, in this structure, more quality leads to less action toward improvements over time.

How to address oscillation is a major theme of this book. Let me give you a flavor of what is to come by turning our attention to how we address this oscillation.

Using Structural Tension to Address the TQM Oscillation

Here is a major point. Drum-roll! Burrrrrrrrrrrr. In the *condition-analysis-adjustment* cycle discussed in the prior section, we can re-design the structure by establishing structural tension. In fact, we must do this, because as discussed earlier, structural conflicts are not problems and so cannot be addressed with a problem-solving approach.

Remembering what we learned about structural tension in Part 1 of this book, we first ask ourselves what do we want to create: What is our desired end result—our vision. This question needs to be considered from a broader perspective than simply "the best quality possible" or "customer satisfaction." Our goals within TQM must be connected to the organization's overall business strategy—to a real strategic business result. If TQM sounding goals are developed in a vacuum, they become meaningless. How does it relate to the broader picture? We need to know.

Once we decide on our vision, we then determine our current reality. And when we have both in mind, we add our TQM techniques to our action plans; part of our action plan includes a condition-analysis-adjustment cycle.

The structural tension motivates a path of least resistance in which the TQM techniques are easily adopted in support of the over-riding goals, rather than something to be resisted or something that runs out of steam as we use it. Here is an illustration of this point.

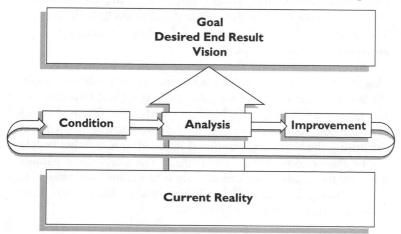

Those organizations that succeed brilliantly at a total quality approach use structural tension whether or not they know it. But when they know how to use structural tension consciously, rather than as part of their "unconscious competence," they can use it even more powerfully. Their systematic improvements become strategic. People are clear about the point. They know the results they are after. Accurate statistical measurements and other instruments of observation and analysis that help tell the story gauge current reality. Rather than arbitrary standards, relevant standards can be used to measure that improvement. The best standard of measurement anyone can use is this: Where are we in relationship to our vision?

Unfortunately, when many organizations use a total quality approach, reengineering or other fundamental change systems, they do so from a problem-solving frame of reference; thus the real advantages of such approaches are barely realized, because the underlying structure leads to oscillation, not to advancement.

United States Air Force Lt. Colonel Larry Willers, of Wright Laboratory, has used both TQM and the structural approach in his work as an in-house trainer and structural consultant. Here is what he had to say:

> As an Air Force laboratory, we knew we needed to continually improve in order to maintain our viability as an organization. We saw Total Quality Management as the way to do it. And we did improve our employee's awareness, interpersonal skills, and understanding of customer focus and process. But we were unable to fundamentally improve the way we conduct business. Our people care about their work and do want to do it better. But they were frustrated that their efforts had made little difference. The reason was that we had made no fundamental change to the structure of our organization.
>
> Once we understood the structural forces in play, we were able to design a structure that clearly moves us toward our goals. We are now focused on our customers' needs and targeting our technology research and TQM efforts within the frame of structural tension. And, we were able to change the structure without disturbing the basic organizational leadership hierarchy. People are in the same positions, reporting to the exact same people, but how they make decisions has been fundamentally altered to support our goals, rather than simply solve problems. It is great to realize you can make real progress.

As we explore the structural approach, it is important to remember that structural dynamics is not a problem-solving technique. It is instead a study of structure that requires an understanding of how structure works and how to redesign our organizations so that the underlying structure supports our aspirations.

Quick Review

Problem Solving and Oscillation

- Problem solving, a common approach toward management, creates an oscillating pattern of behavior because, as problems are solved, the motivation for action is reduced. Then, as action is reduced, the problem grows larger, which increases the motivation for action to reduce it, and then the cycle begins again.

- This oscillation is reflected in the organization's behavior:

  —Actions are initiated in reaction to problems, not to achieve desired results;

  —Actions focus on eliminating problems, not on bringing something into existence;

  —Organizational learning is limited to problems and diminishes as the problems diminish;

  —The organization's focus changes from one problem to another, even if the initial problem remains;

  —Causes (the ultimate problems) can become the organization's primary focus;

  —Problems dictate our actions.

TQM, Problem Solving, and Oscillation

- When TQM or other change systems are used as problem-solving devices, they do not work. As quality improvements are made, the incentive to make further improvements lessens, and the organization moves toward oscillation.

- However, when this cycle is placed into the context of structural tension, it moves toward advancement.

CHAPTER
8

Structural Conflicts of the Rich and Famous

In Chapter 6, we used change versus continuity to illustrate structural conflicts. In this chapter, we are going to describe some of the other major structural conflicts that both senior and middle managers face throughout their organizational lives.

There are two outcomes we hope to achieve in this chapter. One is to be able to recognize these specific structural conflicts in our organizations, because they occur in organizations of all sizes.

Our second goal is to be able to recognize other structural conflicts when we see them. The sixth law of structure states that structural conflicts produce an oscillating pattern of behavior. Thus whenever organizations oscillate, we will be able to find various structural conflicts that are the root cause. Once we can identify other structural conflicts that may exist, we have a better foundation by which to redesign the organization.

We begin by examining a structural conflict that oscillates between growth and capacity and that restricts the organization's success.

The Conflict Between Growth and Capacity

Organizations are in the business of expanding their operation in many ways such as areas/markets, profits, product mix, customer service, scale, and scope. Most managers feel it is their job to grow the company. So why do many organizations experience critical limitations when they attempt to do so? Because there is a structural conflict between growth and capacity in which the path of least resistance is first to drive growth, but later to resist that growth and put limitations on the organization.

Growth Is the Dominant Goal

When growth is the dominant goal, the desire to expand is resolved by growing the company.

But as we grow, we stress the organization's capacity. Growth increases the workload, which will lead to either:

The same number of people doing more work; or

New people being added.

If the same number of people are doing significantly more work, they become less effective. Management may say, "Let's get creative. Take risks! Be empowered! Do something different! Let's reorganize!" hoping that greater productivity will come from the same number of people.

Usually this idea looks good on paper. But, then reality hits, or should we say current reality becomes a factor in the structure. An increased workload does not often lead to new and inventive procedures for two reasons. First, the worst time to ask people to adopt new methods is when they are feeling overwhelmed. They feel they can barely keep up, let alone learn some new cockamamie work method, brought to you by the same people who *increased* your workload.

Second, what about the learning curve associated with adopting new methods? When we learn, we are almost always less efficient before we can learn to be more efficient.

When people are confronted with increasing demands, they tend to lapse into familiar "tried and true" work habits rather than taking on new and unfamiliar methods. Can you blame them?

So let's not give the same number of people more work. Let's add more people. But if we add more people to do extra work, the workload will not decrease instantly, because the new people need to be trained. Who will train them? The very people whose workload has just increased. New people will add to the strain on capacity before they are able to reduce the workload.

It's the same thing when new technology is added. The learning curve needed to master the new systems strains capacity temporarily before it is of any real help.

Limited Capacity Becomes Dominant

In structural conflicts, first one tension-resolution system drives the action, but as that system resolves its tension, another competing system begins to drive the action. The technical term for this is *a shift of dominance*. Even though, good guys that we are, we try to increase capacity, we come up against the current level of capacity, which can seem fixed and unmovable.

Our good intentions strain capacity, leading to a shift in dominance—to the second tension-resolution system in the structural conflict.

Remember, tension comes from a difference, contrast, or discrepancy between two things. The tension driving this second tension-resolution system is the discrepancy between the *actual* capacity of the organization and the *desired amount* of capacity demanded by growth that has taken place.

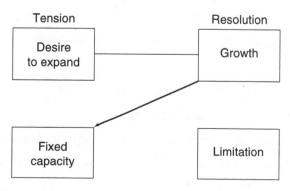

The more growth there is, the more that capacity is strained. Fixed capacity becomes the dominant system, which drives the action, and the path of least resistance for the organization is to limit the growth we wanted to create.

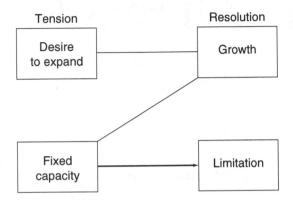

Back to Growth Being Dominant

Once growth is limited by the organization putting a halt to it, strain on capacity decreases and everyone breathes a little easier for a while. But once that second tension-resolution system moves toward resolution, guess what happens. You're right! We begin to think, "We should be growing!" So we oscillate back to square one.

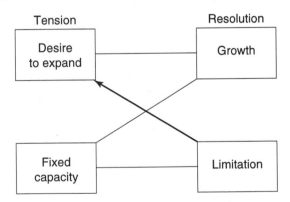

Here is a common pattern in organizations:

People become dedicated to growth.

As the company's workload increases, capacity becomes strained.

Growth slows down as people are forced to shift their attention to managing capacity issues.

Sales versus Manufacturing

Usually, capacity is not fixed in stone, but it takes longer to increase capacity than to produce growth. The lag time functions as if capacity were fixed in stone, or at least fixed at a rate that is too slow for the desired rate of expansion—fixed in molasses. For example, the sales guys are off building sales, but they come up against the limits of manufacturing.

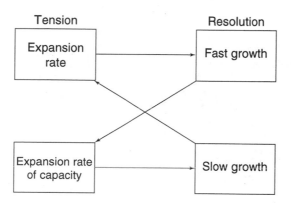

In organizations that have this structural conflict, the salespeople are motivated to build up sales because they get commissions. The more sales, the more commissions. They then need to deliver the product. The strain on the plant creates bigger and bigger time delays. The customers begin to have to wait. They don't like that a bit. They begin to put pressure on their salesperson. The salespeople begin to put pressure on manufacturing. But you can't get blood out of a stone.

So a third or fourth shift is put on and the plant is running at 98% of capacity, and the safety officer is warning everyone to be careful to avoid accidents. The salespeople start showing up at the plant to "escort" their orders through. If they are able to do that, other orders get put on hold, and other customers experience even more delay. Crisis leads to putting limits on the sales volume, and more delays lead the customers to go elsewhere. Sales go down. Commissions go down. But then the sales effort goes up, and the cycle begins again.

The relationship between capacity and growth is a vital element in the overall success of the organization's expansion goals. Unfortunately, most organizations haphazardly set up their sales growth goals independently from their capacity to serve their customers. The forces are in play against each other. The path of least resistance in the structure is to oscillate.

The Conflict Between Business Growth and Profit

In this conflict, we want to invest in order to expand the business, *and* we want to cut costs in order to increase profits. Investment conflicts with cutting costs.

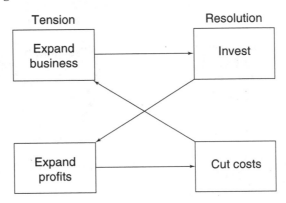

We now layer onto this example the interests of the shareholders. What do investors in stock want? High return on investment.

What does the organization want? Capital to invest in development of the enterprise. But when capital is used for reinvestment, immediate return on investment often goes down, and money available for shareholders' dividends or stock buybacks is reduced until the investment can be recouped by growth.

A conflict of interest develops between the shareholders and the organization, producing oscillation:

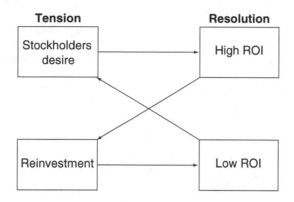

At first, the focus within the organization is growing the business. New plants are built or new technology developed, costing money and time. But no one knows for sure if these additions will increase the company's fortunes, and, as the investment is implemented, profits are lower and the performance of the stock begins to fall; the immediate attractiveness of the stock decreases as the company's future looks unpredictable to Wall Street.

Stock performance affects the organization's cost of capital; money becomes more expensive. Other companies, whose stock is performing better in the market, can borrow money at lower interest rates and enjoy a decisive competitive advantage.

The company begins to look vulnerable, and images of hostile takeovers loom on the horizon. A crisis develops, and senior management is asked to focus on the performance of the stock. The organization reconsiders its position, and begins to work toward making its stock more attractive to the stock market.

The focus shifts from reinvestment in the company to generating higher profit. But after this crisis is over and the stock is performing well again and the company's competitors are no longer threatening, the company reverts to a focus on long-term reinvestment.

This structural conflict will oscillate between short- and long-term strategies as the path of least resistance changes.

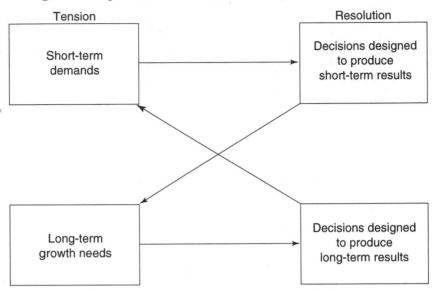

Following the Path of Least Resistance

Let's look at this structural phenomenon from our rubber-band analogy. As we move toward our long-term goals, short-term demands increase tension on the opposing rubber band. In fact, notice that the most tension is in the short-term rubber band. Where is it easier for us to go in this structure? The path of least resistance is in the direction of the short-term demands that require our immediate attention.

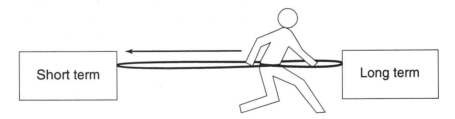

We jump into action. We do the only thing that nature will allow us to do. We follow the path of least resistance. We take whatever action necessary to satisfy the short-term demands. But then, there is another shift of dominance. The long-term rubber band kicks in. Now, where is it easier for us to go? The path of least resistance leads us back to long-term strategy.

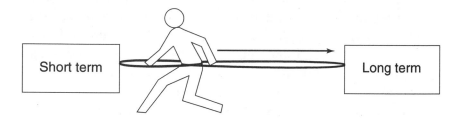

In this structural conflict, as in all others, it seems as if the organization has a lot of trouble making up its mind. Does it want to develop its long-range plans? Or is it in the business of selling stock? Senior management's oscillating behavior between these two points can lead to appalling decisions that undermine morale and organizational alignment. This is the kind of thing that drives people crazy, because it's hard for them to do their jobs and support the organization, which they deeply want to do. Leadership can seem flaky, and then leaders lose credibility. Once that happens, it's hard for them to get it back.

Many Western corporations have fallen victim to this structure as companies have merged, been acquired, changed management, changed direction, and even changed industries.

This structure is less dominant in some of the great companies such as Sony, Nike, Microsoft, and even smaller companies that seem not to be subject to this type of oscillation. Why? Because long-term planning produces structural tension as the key organizing principle, and conflicts of interests are managed within the frame of knowing what the senior goals are, what current reality is, and what the strategies are to move from the actual state to the desired state.

Conflicts Stemming from the "New Management Style"

We hear a lot about new management style these days. Cross-functional teams are said to break down the walls of miscommunication and encourage people to think more systemically. Decision making is being pushed down further into the organization, becoming decentralized, transforming the autocratic management tyrants into consensual types who will listen, communicate, share their feelings, and empower their people.

Once-proprietary information is now readily distributed throughout the organization. As stock options are made available to members of the organization, they are encouraged to think of themselves as owners. Managers are also encouraged to treat their people with dignity and respect, and the employee's health and general well-being are promoted as a high value that will lead to company loyalty.

All of these trends sound enlightened, indeed. Yet, when many organizations attempt to implement these practices, the byproduct is often confusion and instability.

A common complaint of senior management is that people don't make the decisions they have been given the authority to make. Another is that, although cross-functional teams have productive work sessions, their actual plans tend to be put on hold. Though members are encouraged to think from a wider organizational perspective, they still think and act out of their own local concerns. With all the talk about how people should be treated and how they should act, political intrigues still dominate the scene. Why are these good ideas about management style not always as useful as they should be?

Answer: The structural conflict between decentralization and centralization determine an organization's behavior more than all the words and good thoughts in the world.

Decentralization versus Centralization

The change from centralized to decentralized management was more radical than it might seem at first glance. Decisions are a medium of power. By pushing decisions down into the organization, power is being distributed more widely. More power everywhere means less power concentrated in the hands of a few. This did not sit well with everybody. Those who were very successful in their careers as managers succeeded by knowing how to make decisions. They kept control in their own hands so that things were being done "properly." When decision making was decentralized, successful managers were asked to relinquish some of their control. Many of them found this hard to do.

Managers take their responsibility to assure their group's success seriously. If the power to do a good job is taken away from them, they become a little insecure. Others may make the wrong decisions, or not make decisions strategically. Things can go terribly wrong, and the manager may find out too late to correct it.

Here is the structural conflict faced by the managers and those they managed.

But the manager may lack vital information that people closer to the situation confront daily. This leads to a desire to have the people in the trenches authorized to make immediate and timely decisions.

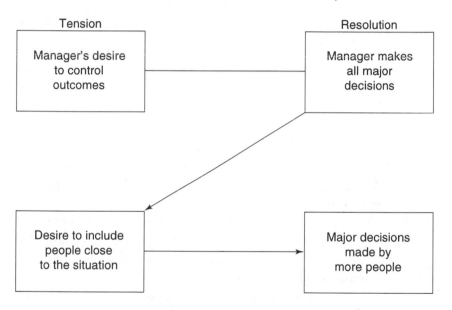

But when more people make more decisions, the manager has less control, and the consequences may not be what the manager wants. This situation feels awfully unstable to many managers. Pressure builds. Soon, the manager's desire to control the outcome becomes the dominant factor in the structure again, and he or she reclaims the power to make all major decisions and breathes a sigh of relief—until the next time thorough in the cycle.

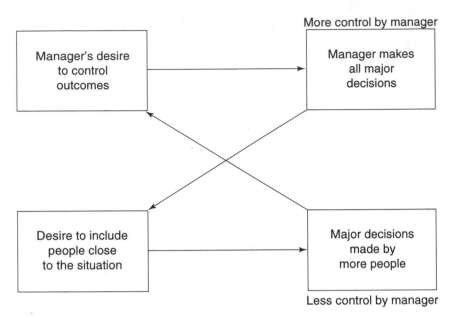

More people making decisions leads to less control. Fewer people making decisions leads to more control. The result is an oscillation between centralized and decentralized decision making.

Decision-Making Power versus Fear of Failure

And what about the people who are given this new power to decide? We would expect them to seize the opportunity of playing a bigger role in their organization.

Surprisingly, they often do not grab the bull by the horns, but rather, they become awfully shy. Many people become uncomfortable with their new-found power, and they avoid making decisions they have been empowered to make. Why?

When we are given the decision-making power, we also are given the accountability. We may fail. The Surgeon General has determined that failure can be hazardous to your corporate health.

Most organizations do not know how to deal with failure judiciously. Failure is usually an unforgivable mistake that leads to punishment of one sort or another. When that's the case, everyone avoids making mistakes. Why put your neck in a noose? Because the potential threat of failure goes up proportionally with the degree of power, people are less likely than ever before to make decisions.

Here is a structural look at the phenomenon:

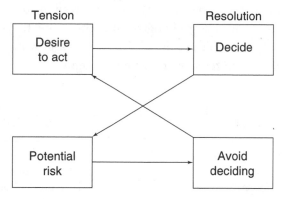

People want to play an important role in their organizations. But, when they begin to make decisions, their risk increases. They resolve the risk by avoiding decisions that are potentially threatening. From the structure, we begin to understand why people seem to be behaving in inconsistent ways. The underlying structure is generating an oscillating path of least resistance. People are responding quite naturally to a built-in conflict within the organization.

Structural Conflicts Are Everywhere

Structural conflicts do not exist only in large companies, nor do they involve only company-wide issues and senior management. They are pervasive in the world of organizations.

An R&D Conflict

In a high-tech multinational firm, the R&D managers had a mandate to do applied research, which was one of the company's major core competitive advantages. Research was respected and seen as time and money well spent. This produced the following tension and resolution:

But halfway through the research cycle, the team was told to create more products. After all, they were not only a research team, but a product development team, as well. And the more time the team spent on research activities, the more the people responsible for products felt they were being short-changed, and the more they feared that their mandates wouldn't get done. There was a growing conflict between the competing tension-resolution systems:

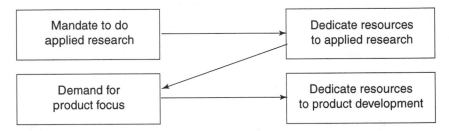

Of course, once the R&D managers had shifted their focus to product development, their internal customers began to feel insecure about their mandates and put the pressure on the team to go back to research.

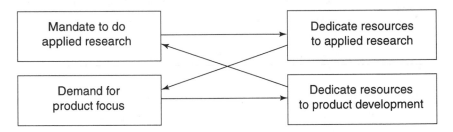

It's easy to see the oscillating behavior over time and its causes. And we can guess that the team probably did not satisfy either of its customers.

Nursing School Conflict

In a school of nursing, the students needed clinical and other types of hands-on training. And for this training to be of a high quality, small student-staff ratios are essential. But the state legislature created a system called "weighted credit hours." The legislature funds the university by calculating how many of these credit hours the school can produce: More credit hours, more money. The way to build up the credit hours is more students per instructor. A large class would give more credit hours than clinical study. This put the school of nursing in a structural conflict between funding and quality of education:

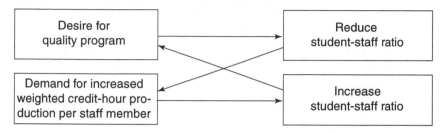

As one tension-resolution system resolved, the other one became dominant, and quality was pitted against getting proper funding.

Small Company Conflict

A small company wanted to expand its expertise, so it hired outside consultants to advise it. But, as the company received more advice, its management felt less in control of the business. So, management rejected the advice and fired the experts. But later, realizing that it needed advice, the company hired experts and. . . .

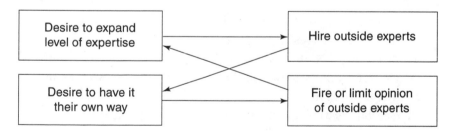

In each example discussed so far in this chapter, there was a single structural conflict. Real life, however, is never that simple, as we shall now see.

Layers of Structural Conflicts

In real life, there isn't just one or two structural conflicts driving the organization to ping-pong back and forth. There are many going on at the same time. The growth-stability conflict often coexists with the change-continuity conflict. Add to this other structural conflicts such as investment versus cutting costs and decentralized versus centralized decision making, and you have a real mess.

Here is an example of multiple structural conflicts working together.

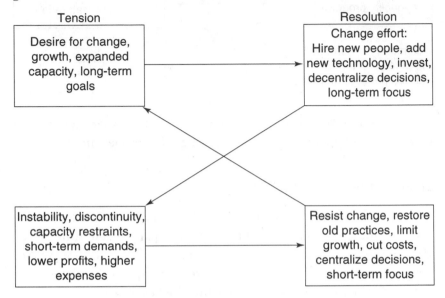

When several structural conflicts operate simultaneously, there is often an experience of desperate struggle as people fight against something that seems beyond their control. They begin to feel resignation and hopelessness. Nothing works and fate, more than imagination and diligence, seems likely to decide the company's future. And whimsical fate is not always kind.

Exacerbating this situation is that these oscillating patterns are hard to see at first because they move so slowly or over a long period of time. But while they may take several years to repeat, people still feel the shifts in the oscillating pattern.

New leadership may temporarily suspend the collective experience of fatalism, but if the structure remains unchanged, the honeymoon with the new CEO will soon be over and people will return to a profound sense of powerlessness. Only this time it is even worse than before, because a glimmer of hope has proven to be merely an illusion.

Management may try to shake the organization out of this malaise with positive motivational furor: "C'mon, everyone! We can do it! We only need to believe in ourselves! Let's sing the company song!"

Or, management may try a "slap in the face" approach with warnings about the negative consequences that will come if the organization doesn't snap out of it.

But carrots and sticks cannot change inadequate structures. Before you get too depressed, remember hope is on the way. And another reminder: We need to understand oscillation and what causes it before we can redesign the structure, generating a new path of least resistance to organizational advancement—in other words, true success.

Identifying Structural Conflicts

Many of the structural conflicts explored in this chapter are found in many organizations, but can we begin to recognize the ones that we haven't talked about? Yes, but we need to look, study, and analyze the organization from a structural point of view.

First, look for oscillating patterns. Look for a situation in which "first we did this . . . and then we did that . . . but then we did this again." You will find them, particularly if your time frame broadens to many months or even years. Here are some questions that may help you:

- What is the first swing in the oscillating pattern?

- As the organization begins to move in that direction, what is the shift away from that swing?

- What are people talking about at first? Then, later, what are they talking about? Has the topic of conversation changed around the company?

Remember: A tension is formed by the discrepancy or difference between two elements—often a desired state in contrast to a current state. As that tension-resolution system moves toward resolution, notice how it exacerbates the tension in the competing system. This will help you understand the behavior you are observing.

Use the following form to describe the structural conflict you are seeing:

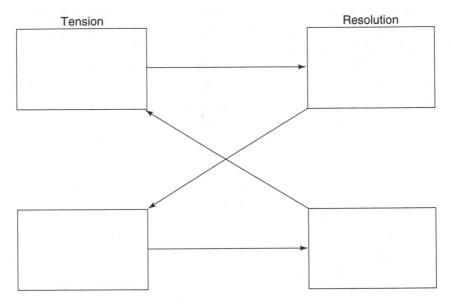

Tension

Resolution

Once you understand the structural conflicts that drive an oscillating pattern, you can begin a real dialogue with your colleagues. But you can talk structure rather than symptom. This makes it easier for everyone to explore the situation without getting defensive or thinking that they have to uphold their department's point of view. Everyone can become more objective. This process is tremendously useful.

While structural conflicts fill the organizational landscape, we are not stuck with them. So get ready! The next chapter introduces the key principle that enables us to redesign organizations so as to eliminate structural conflicts.

Quick Review

- Organizations oscillate because of structural conflicts, and insights can be gained by examining some of the more common ones.

- Organizations oscillate between:

  —Expansion and limitation

  —Strained workload and budgetary constraints—Profit goals and expansion goals

  —Investment and cost cutting

  —Stock performance and reinvestment

  —Short-term and long-term demands

  —Desire to control and desire to include others in decision making

  —Desire to act and potential risk

  —Growth and stability

- Layers of structural conflicts combine to create a wider magnitude of oscillation.

By observing examples of oscillation in your own organization, you can begin to describe the competing tension-resolution systems that form the structural conflict. You can then better understand the structural forces in play and begin a useful dialogue with colleagues.

How to Address Structural Conflicts
The Key to Structural Redesign

Structural conflicts are not problems to be solved but structures that need to be redesigned. This short chapter will give you the key principle in redesigning structural conflicts—that of hierarchy. Then, in Part 3 of this book, we go into greater detail about the elements of organizational design.

The DDD Corporation Revisited

Chapter 6 discussed the structural conflict of the DDD Corporation: change versus continuity. Let's revisit this example to see how to handle the situation. Here is the structural conflict:

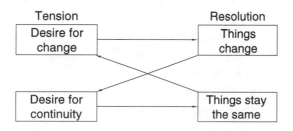

Tension

Desire for change

Desire for continuity

Resolution

Things change

Things stay the same

A desire for change leads to change, which then leads to a desire for continuity, which then leads to avoidance of change. But once continuity has been reestablished, the desire for change reemerges.

What we need is structural tension in the place of the structure conflict. How do we redesign the structure so that's the case?

The DDD management team must first identify what it really wants: What is the desired outcome? In this case, DDD wants two outcomes. It wants change and it also wants continuity. But to the degree that management changed the organization, the continuity was lost. And to the degree that management held on to continuity, its change effort was resisted. How can management address this dilemma?

Hierarchy of Importance

While both goals were important to the company, one goal will be more important to DDD than the other:

> - **Change may be more important than continuity, or**
> - **Continuity may be more important than change**

DDD's management team must create a *hierarchy of importance*. In other words, it must determine which of the two goals is more important. It needs to pick one.

Once it chooses either change or continuity as more important, the next step for DDD is to establish a new structure—establish structural tension by understanding the goal, understanding the current reality, and then constructing an action plan out of that.

What is the goal that DDD actually wants? In the change-continuity example, change itself is a process, not a real result. What result is this process designed to serve? Before DDD can create a hierarchy, it must know what it will have in place after the change has been accomplished. What is DDD trying to achieve through its change campaign? To improve its products? Its management systems? Its relationship with suppliers? To grow its market share? Develop customer loyalty? Or, become more efficient and effective?

Let's say the answer is yes, DDD wants all of those things. Who wouldn't? The question is, would DDD put up with a period of discontinuity to accomplish the change?

Let's think this through for DDD. If change became the senior goal, then DDD must be ready to live with discontinuity—perhaps a high level of discontinuity. From a management point of view, it can prepare the organization for what it will take to accomplish the change. Management will create structural tension, in which successful change is the goal and reality is the current situation unchanged; and one of the action steps it will take is to *manage discontinuity*.

Of course, DDD would rather not have any discontinuity. But it just may come with the territory along with change, so DDD had better face reality.

Organizations are in the habit of constructing strategies for change without considering the degree of continuity they want to maintain while the change effort is being implemented. How much continuity do we need to maintain? How much discontinuity can we live with? Once DDD answers these questions, it can understand the relationship between change and continuity.

Since the desire for change leads to a departure from the norm, DDD's continuity goal will be formed by its change goal—the more change, the less continuity. However, DDD may find that the change goal is impossible to achieve in the short run because the resulting discontinuity may work against the company. This situation provides DDD with an opportunity to rethink its desires.

Which is more important to management:

> - **Fast change that may be disruptive to the organization; or**
> - **Slower change that will help maintain a consistent level of continuity?**

If DDD needs to accomplish its change in a strategic time frame because that is crucial to its success, it will choose to pursue its change goal, knowing full well that continuity will be undermined. Of course, DDD would not want a prolonged period of discontinuity, but management may decide to live with it temporarily.

In this case, the *change* goal is senior to the *continuity* goal.

If the change goal does not need to be accomplished immediately, DDD might decide to build a firm base of organizational continuity, paving the way for the transition before attempting drastic change. In this case, the continuity goal will be senior to the change goal, and

DDD will regulate change by measuring it against adequate continuity, so that the senior goal—continuity—never goes out of an acceptable level.

Continuity Over Change: A Case Study

Let's illustrate the hierarchy of importance with a case study. In order to increase their sales volume, the sales and marketing departments of a large pharmaceutical company formulated a plan to change their marketing approach radically. Instead of a single nationwide strategy with each product line marketed to doctors by a product-specific sales force, they proposed to use fewer salespeople selling a greater variety of products and to develop local marketing strategies tailored to each geographical area. Their idea was based on two major considerations: (1) that each area of the country had a unique consumer mix (Florida, for example, has a larger elderly population than most other parts of the country), and (2) that doctors do not like to be besieged by salespeople.

The sales and marketing departments were enthusiastic about their ideas, and they held a meeting with senior management to propose the plan. Senior management rejected it almost immediately— not because the idea was poorly conceived, but because it was unwilling to adopt an unknown and untested marking strategy over one that was generating the company's major revenue source.

The change might have worked brilliantly, but management did not want to put the economic continuity of the business in jeopardy.* Its interest in continuity was greater than its interest in change, even though the change was designed to increase sales volume. Change in the marketing strategy would need to be organized in the context of economic continuity and to utilize such things as pilot programs in selected regions or single experiments to study the efficacy of the strategy.

---

*Many organizations have damaged their economic base by managing change haphazardly. The relationship with customers can suffer when products are changed or services are disrupted. There are many examples. The most famous example of this disruptive change is when Coke changed its formula, and consumers were outraged. When Jaguar changed the classic curvaceous lines of its XJ6 sedan and gave it a boxy nondescript design, customers felt betrayed.

We Must Choose

Either change or continuity can predominate, but they *cannot* be equal. Therefore, it is necessary to determine which is the more important value. Once we do that, we have created a hierarchy. We have determined our primary goal. Our primary goal will be the focal point in organizing structural tension, and the other goal or goals will be designed to support it.

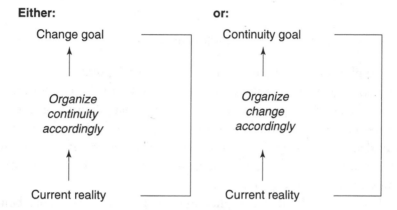

When we move from structural conflict to structural tension, we are defining our more important objective, our primary goal. The goal in the competing tension-resolution system is then reorganized to be supportive of the primary goal, rather than conflicting with it. In other words, if change is primary, putting up with a degree of discontinuity is our secondary choice—we will manage the resulting discontinuity that may occur to support our change effort.

If continuity is primary, then we will minimize our change effort as our secondary choice—we will manage any change efforts to minimize significant disruption.

Once we know our primary desired outcomes, we are able to organize competing outcomes accordingly.

The Drive for Equilibrium

When a structure contains two competing tension-resolution systems and we redesign it into a structure containing only one dominant tension-resolution system, we can describe this change from the standpoint of equilibrium. Remember *structure seeks equilibrium.*

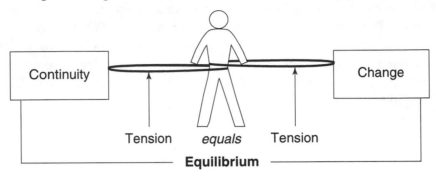

Equilibrium is the point of balance—the midpoint—between two competing goals. But in the case of structural tension, equilibrium is created when the current situation and the desired situation are the same—like, we have what we want! This point is absolutely essential in understanding why the path of least resistance in some structures leads toward the complete achievement of our goals, and in other structures leads us to oscillation.

Let's think about the implications of the structure's goal being equilibrium. When the structure accomplishes its goal, the dynamic is over. There is no longer a tendency to move from one condition to another. The structure comes into a resolved or relaxed mode. There is no tension any longer.

Now, the kicker. Let's look at the same situation—you have achieved the result you want, but now it is in the context of structural conflict; you have a very different structural dynamic in play. Having what you want in structural conflict is the point in the structure in which there is *highest* state of nonequilibrium. It is the point in the structure that the structure wants to adjust itself and move away from the nonequilibrium state.

> • **Within structural conflict, having what you want is the point of *most* nonequilibrium.**
> • **Within structural tension, having what you want is the point of *perfect* equilibrium.**

In one structure, having what you want leads you away from having what you want. In the other structure, it does not.

Think of it this way: In structural conflict, there are two rubber bands stretched around your waist, each pulling you with equal strength toward two competing goals. When you reach your goal, one rubber band is fully strained, pulling you back toward its goal. The path of least resistance wants to ease the tension, and, therefore, you end up moving away from your success. This is why "success cannot succeed in an organization that oscillates" is an inescapable law of organizational structure.

When you create a relationship of hierarchy between the competing goals, you are assigning one goal to the desired end result section of structural tension, and the other an action step that supports the more important goal. The tendency for the structural conflict itself may be placed into current reality, as in: Current reality including "we want both competing goals which are mutually exclusive," and the desired end result is: "we pick this one as more important." When you establish this kind of hierarchy, metaphorically, you are moving from a rocking chair into a car.

From Structural Conflict to Structural Tension

Given what we said above, when we discover structural conflicts running rampant all over the organization, we can charge into our design mode and establish structural tension. Within the context of structural conflicts, we can establish a hierarchy between the two competing tensions. We can choose one of the two competing goals as more important. We designate the competing one as subordinate.

Let's illustrate this using the growth-stability structural conflict:

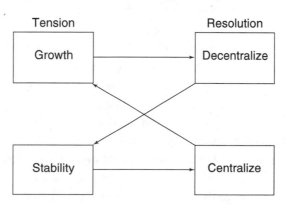

In this case, decentralized decision making intended to promote growth conflicts with the organization's stability, and the centralized decision making intended to achieve stability conflicts with growth, particularly in spreading the management burden throughout the organization.

Once we determine which is more important to us, stability or growth, this structural conflict can be converted into structural tension. Then we can redesign the structure by establishing goals that reflect our hierarchy of values. We can then support it managerially by the decisions we make.

Most structural conflicts in organizations can be addressed by establishing hierarchies. That process addresses specific structural conflicts that may exist, but it doesn't tell us how to build an organization that advances, builds, and breeds success on success. In Part 3, we dive into the waters of redesigning the organization so that the path of least resistance moves us to build the kind of high-performance organization we want. How do we create new structures that support our aims, our aspirations, our ambitions, and our purpose?

Making the Hard Choices

How can an organization support its actual vision and direction in light of the many pressures it faces from various structural conflicts?

Too often, people in senior management positions in the organization fail to make the hard choices. They might attempt to "balance" competing factors, such as long-term growth investment strategies and short-term financial performance, but these choices neutralize each other, and it is impossible for the organization to serve either one adequately.

The organization needs to determine which of the competing factors is the most important and then support that one over the others. Not everyone will be happy with the choice, but it must be made and then reinforced by the series of secondary decisions that support it. The organization must take a stand for the chosen direction.

When it is necessary to take a stand, some people in senior roles avoid the "moment of truth" and attempt diplomacy instead. If an organization does not decide which competing goals are the most important, none of the goals will be adequately satisfied or supported.

Members of the organization will not know how to address the many critical issues they face. Each side of the structural conflict will think its approach is the correct one. They will think that if the other side were more understanding of the "real situation," there would be agreement to support the "correct" approach (which happens to be their own approach).

As a consequence of weak senior management leadership, the organization is left directionless and everyone suffers.

In one pharmaceutical company, for example, senior management failed to decide whether to support virology research as its R&D strategy. Some members of the company thought much of the future success of the business lay in virology, but others thought their competitors had a better command of virology research; just to play catch-up would be an enormous investment, putting them in a "me too" position without market or scientific superiority or control.

The issue was discussed endlessly, but no real decision was ever made. Virology looked like a good bet some months and a bad one other months. People in research continued to explore virology compounds. When they had developed something that was ready to enter the FDA clinical-trial process, the clinical group responsible for the trials was unprepared to handle the workload. They didn't have the staff, the funding, or, as far as they knew, the corporate mandate. A conflict developed between the R&D department and clinical research. At first the cause of the conflict appeared to be personality problems between rival groups of strong-willed scientists. To people in clinical research, the R&D people seemed like a group of mavericks who were manipulating the system; to the R&D people, clinical research seemed to be thwarting their important work. Conflict-resolution techniques were tried, but, as we might expect, they failed to address the real issue.

The real issue was this: Because of the leadership vacuum that developed because senior managers didn't make a hierarchical choice, people created their own sense of direction based on their understanding of what the corporation was trying to accomplish. Each side in this dispute continued to wonder why the other side was being so unreasonable and uncooperative. Until this issue was driven upward, forcing senior management to make a final decision about virology, the conflict was unaddressable.

This example points to a chronic pattern within many corporations. The senior managers fail to set adequate direction, so people in other levels of the organization compensate by setting their own direction. The results always lead to structural oscillation.

This is because of the eighth law of organizational structure.

The **EIGHTH** Law of Organizational Structure

When a senior organizing principle is absent, the organization will oscillate. When a senior organizing principle is dominant, the organization will advance.

Without a higher-order organizing principle, such as structural tension, in which the company's aspirations and values are positioned in relationship to its current reality, an organization will self-organize into various structural conflicts. Why? Because various groups try to do a good job, and so, they support the effort they see as the "correct one."

Even cross-functional teams cannot help create advancement when an organizing principle is absent. The attempt will be neutralized because they will find they don't have true organizational support. Department heads will be caught right in the middle of a juicy structural conflict. The consequence will be a return to structural oscillation.

But with a senior organizing principle such as the company's values and aspirations, the organization can easily create structural tension. Members can see reality objectively and they can develop effective action plans that create momentum. They can translate the various structural conflicts they discover into structural tension by sorting out hierarchy, and they can redesign the path of least resistance so they can advance.

The next few chapters will help you to identify the organizational purpose and create business and management strategies using structural tension—the structure that has the right path of least resistance.

Quick Review

- Establishing a hierarchy between competing goals is the key to structural redesign.

- When we move from structural conflict to structural tension, we are defining our primary goal. This action reorganizes the relationship between competing goals.

- This is a change from a structure that contains two competing tension-resolution systems to a structure that contains only one dominant tension-resolution system.

- In an oscillating structure, the fulfillment of a desire produces a high state of nonequilibrium. In a resolving structure, the fulfillment of a desire produces a state of equilibrium.

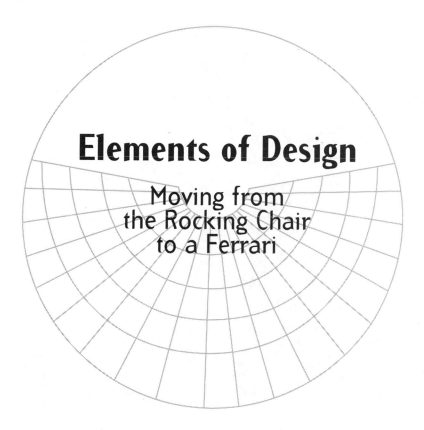

PART 3

Elements of Design

Moving from the Rocking Chair to a Ferrari

CHAPTER
10

Purpose
What Unifies the Organization

What the Heck Are We Doing This For?

Why do we have an organization? Before we begin to talk about share-holders' return on investment and money, money, money, let's look more deeply and honestly at why we exist as an organization. As there is more to life than making a buck, there is more to an organization than making a buck. Making a buck is vital. I wish you all the bucks you want. But when we say that the organization's reason to exist is *simply* money, we miss the point. It hardly ever is that simple. Organizations exist for many reasons. They have purposes, often good and great ones.

I am not trying to imply that every organization has a profound purpose that is worthy of Mother Teresa. But often the organization's purpose is a lot deeper than people give it credit for.

If the organization has a purpose but acts in ways that contradict its purpose, it will produce structural conflicts. The path of least resistance will lead to oscillation. Organizations, like people, suffer when they are not being true to themselves.

The Dynamism of Purpose

Organizations can be great because through them people can join together and accomplish feats that would be impossible for any individual to achieve alone. Thanks to organizations, miracle drugs are created that save people's lives, technology is developed that empowers people to communicate and create, services are offered that enable people to accomplish their work, products are made that enrich us all. Through organizations, roads are built, skyscrapers erected, electricity and water distributed, food made available, and economic growth advanced. Organizations are the central civilizing force of our age.

But we must remind ourselves that organizations are not an organic phenomenon of nature. They are a refined human invention. We create organizations. Like many creations, once they exist, they begin to have a life of their own. They grow, develop, reach young adulthood, middle age, and even old age. But unlike our own life cycle, they can be reborn, renew themselves, and become young again and start over.

So what is the organization's reason to exist? The answer to that question varies, depending on the organization. Each organization has its own particular purpose in its life. Some organizations have very good purposes. Some organizations have truly great purposes. Some have lackluster reasons to exist. Not all organizational purposes are created equal.

The founders of the company implant the organization's purpose into its genetic code. Later, people joined the organization and contributed new aspects and dimensions to it. They added to it, focused it, and aimed it. The purpose developed. The purpose often continues to develop.

"Spiritual Purpose"

Many organizations have what we could think of as their "spiritual purpose"—"spiritual" not in the sense of religion, but in the sense of the tangible spirit or essence of organization; spiritual in the sense of a kind of higher calling for the organization. Within those organizations, we feel the purpose by what excites us, by the organization's true values and aspirations, and by the services and products that the organization generates.

We also recognize the purpose by what disappoints us about the organization—its failure to live up to its values, the compromises it makes, its contradictions, and its inability to live up to its potential.

When I think of a company that had a tremendous sense of purpose but then lost its bearings, I think of Apple Computer. I love Apple Computer. That is to say, I love Macintoshes. So, I was particularly saddened when Apple went through a down period in which it seemed to lose its way. It can be a great company again, but only if it roots itself in its founding purpose (although, not its founding business, because the industry has changed many times since Steve Jobs and Steve Wozniak first entered that famous garage where it all began). When Apple regains that first blush of excitement, that lump in the throat, that "it's so good you can't stand it," it will be back on track.

One of the best examples of an organization that is consistently true to its purpose is Nike. Nike is large—$9 billion in revenues. It dominates the athletic shoe market worldwide, it is a major factor in promoting sports, and it is itself an incredible phenomenon. What makes Nike so different? I think it is Nike's "spiritual purpose," which is rooted in its authentic dedication and love of sports. But Nike has been greatly misunderstood and, because of its success, has become an easy target for cheap shots.

Speaking of cheap shots, recently *60 Minutes* did a feature about kids who are future basketball stars and the training and support that companies like Nike gives them. There was Leslie Stahl, trying to imply that all Nike is doing is exploiting innocent young talents, and the point of that is, as she put it, "To sell high-priced sneakers." Actually, what Nike and the other companies are doing is giving kids a chance to pursue their dreams. But many cynical media types have trouble knowing a good thing when they see it.

If the folks at *60 Minutes* took the time and trouble to find out the facts, they would have studied how Nike makes its decisions.

The people at Nike make decisions that are guided by how they can advance the cause of sports. For example, if they could sell more "sneakers" by producing a stylish looking shoe that didn't have proper sports related engineering in it, they wouldn't do it, no matter how much money they could make. Period, end of story.

Nike spends enormous amounts of money perfecting the design aspects of their products. The average consumer is not aware of many of these innovations—that is, until he or she begins to use the products. Nike's management team includes many young, dedicated managers who, for the most part, are themselves accomplished athletes. These people love sports, and they care about the athletes and consumers who use their products.

In Nike, we see an example of an organization that is consistently true to its higher purpose, and we see a company that is having a very positive impact on the lives of people in its target markets. Yes, Leslie, they sell shoes, as well as other related sports products, and they do a damn good job doing it. But the great underlying strength that enables Nike to rise above many other companies in the same field is its "spiritual purpose" that penetrates everything it does.

Of course, like all companies, Nike has had its problems; some of them based on market conditions, some of them on fads that come and go, some of them based on having chosen the wrong subcontractors, which made it seem as if the company sanctioned poor working conditions, which it doesn't. But Nike always bounces back, because it is an organization of people who are dedicated and aligned to their purpose.

There are many other great companies that organize themselves by their "spiritual purpose": Sony, Amazon.Com, Walt Disney, Dream Works, Virgin Air, and many companies that are known mostly within their industries. These companies are good examples of what organizations *can* be. None of them are perfect, but perfection doesn't make a good or great organization.

Well Beyond Words

The difficulty with talking about the organization's purpose is that it mostly exists on some level that's beyond words. We can feel it, sense it, intuit it, and align to it, but most anything we say about it sounds dumb. This is like many other important aspects of our lives. Love is real and tangible. You know when you are in love and you know when you love. But it's awfully hard to talk about. Imagine saying to your significant other, "I love you because of your smile." Does that mean that on days in which your significant other forgets to smile, you won't love him or her? Imagine telling your kids, "I love you because you did a great job with your homework." We love our children, and whenever we try to put the reason into words, we sound like idiots. We know we love them—we can't say exactly why.

The same is true when it comes to the organization's most meaningful organizing principle. We can feel an organization's purpose, but whenever we open our mouth to express it, the words come out like chopped liver:

> We are the company that has the most advanced technology in widget design, is recognized for being the industry leader in quality, has high market share with totally satisfied loyal customers, in an environment where people are able to develop their talents and abilities by meeting the challenges of today and tomorrow, while producing extremely high profitability.

This is not the kind of statement that you can feel in the guts.

For years now, organizations have thought it was important to write mission, purpose, and vision statements. The team goes to the mountain (really the closed-in, stuffy, hotel room) and writes it. But before words reach flipchart, the team has a very valuable discussion. Members ask themselves very good questions such as: Who are we? What are we trying to accomplish? Why are we trying to do it? The interaction among the group can be wonderfully insightful. The people in the room may get to the point where they actually feel the spirit of the organization. But, in the act of trying to express what they feel, they inadvertently do a disservice to the purpose. They trivialize it by trying to write down.

When they come out of the room, they have this silly statement that only they really get. They were there when they put it together, so they know what it's trying to say. The trouble is, people who weren't in the room, and who didn't share that experience, read the statement. The statement they read is silly. They know it doesn't describe what they feel about the organization. They try to like it, but, try as they may, they just don't.

The statement then goes up on the walls, or on plaques, or on little cards that everyone is supposed to carry around in their wallets. The more the statement exists, the more everyone realizes that nobody is making decisions based on it. The reality that they see around them contradicts the statement, and, over time, the statement seems more and more idiotic.

The funny thing is that the instinct to write a statement is on the right track. The hope that we have when we write these statements is to tie the organization together by a common theme. We look for a unifying principle—in other words, a way of having all the members of the organization understand the fundamental reason that the organization exists, so they can do two very important things: (1) See if the purpose matches their own personal and professional purpose. When the individual's purpose is aligned with the organization's purpose, there is great possibility for mutual benefit; (2) Take independent action, which better fits into the aims of the organization. People can be more effective and work better with others when everyone understands what we, as an organization, are trying to accomplish.

Matching Our Actions with Our Purpose

The instinct is right, but the technique is all wrong. The greatest poets have trouble putting their most meaningful ideas into words. Why do we think a bunch of managers is going to be any better at it?

The instinct to have everyone in the organization tied together with a common purpose and direction is what we, as managers, are trying to accomplish. The fact is that there are better and more direct ways of bring people together with a common aim than writing statements. The first is the actual reality of the purpose. If the organization has a "spiritual" purpose, does it express it in the decisions it makes? Of course, all organizations do and don't make decisions in ways that are consistent with their purpose, but the real question is, "What's the pattern?" If most of the time they do, then people come to understand the purpose without ever being told. If the answer is that most of the time decisions are made in ways that are inconsistent with their purpose, then no amount of statements in the world are going to convince people that the company is guided by its higher calling. That's not to say it doesn't have a higher calling or "spiritual purpose." What disappoints and frustrates people often points to the contradiction between reality and their purpose, aspirations, and values.

While most organizations have a purpose statement, a vision statement, or mission statement, very few have the clarity of vision, purpose, or mission to guide their decisions and actions. Which would we rather work for, a company that had a purpose statement but didn't have a purpose, or a company that had a purpose but didn't have a purpose statement? Of course we would all choose the real thing over the propaganda. But even an organization that has a true purpose can rob that purpose of its power by reducing it to a slogan.

When I work with clients, we hardly ever talk about their purpose. But, their purpose is very present in the work that we do together. It is imbedded in all of the strategic planning, in all of the management design work, and in the business that supports the products and services that they offer. In some organizations, you can get it when you walk through the halls, or in overhearing conversations, or in watching people work together.

Once in a while, a few people try to deny that their organization has a "spiritual purpose" or any other purpose other than just to crank out money. They may say, "Our purpose is return on investment" or "Profit" or "Enhancing shareholders' value." They have deadened themselves to the deeper essence of the organization. Money plays an important role in the life of an organization, including nonprofit and governmental organizations. Without adequate money, you don't get to "do your purpose." But is money the real goal? If we took the same investment the organization represents and put the money in a high-yield account, would we do better in terms of profit? How about the right combination of stocks? Often, the answer is yes; we could make more money in other ways than through the work of the organization. Even when the answer is no, there are usually other ways to make more profit more easily than the hard work it takes.

Doing Something That Matters

The people who claim that return on investment is the purpose usually do not sell the company and put the money in a bank or some other form of investment.

There is in each of us a dynamic urge to build, grow, aspire, and create. Not all of us have this urge to the same intensity. Not all of us have the same desires or aspirations. But we surely can observe that we possess such deep urges. We would rather be doing something important than something unimportant. We would rather be involved with something that matters than with something that doesn't.

At their root, most organizations have something special, something quite human. It is the instinct to do something that matters.

Think about your own life. Do you have a higher purpose of some kind? Does the work that you do match your life's purpose? This question is better answered once you understand the "spiritual purpose" of your organization. For most people, there is a direct match between their own values, aspirations, and sense of purpose and that of the organization. But for most people, this match goes on unrecognized. If the match is there, there is a possibility for great mutual benefit—organization and member. If it happens not to be there for you, think about other situations that would be more conducive to real alignment between the organization's purpose and your own.

Purpose is not an empty or abstract ideal. For the purpose to be real, we need to make it viable. How can we express the purpose in reality? That is the function of the business strategy. That's next!

Quick Review

- An organization's fundamental structural tension is the difference between the way that it wants to act and the way that it is currently acting—the difference between the desired expression and the current expression of its purpose.

- The desired organizational purpose answers the question, "Why do we exist as an organization?"

- When an organization's actions contradict its desired purpose, the organization will oscillate.

- An organization's purpose is not fixed; it continues to grow and develop over time.

- Purpose cannot be put into words; it is a sense of spirit within the organization that excites us about the organization's aspirations and actions. Thus, mission, purpose, and vision statements tend at best to trivialize, and at worst, distort, an organization's purpose.

Business Strategy

The Path of Least Resistance
to Our Purpose

An organization's purpose is its cornerstone—its foundation. How do we build the organization upon it? How do we support it? How do we create the path of least resistance that leads to the fulfillment of our purpose?

This is done through the organization's business strategy. We need to build a *business* around the purpose. If we don't, the purpose won't have an opportunity to be put into practice. Business, in this sense, is a broader concept than only commercial, for-profit companies. That is one part of business, but it also includes questions of how the funding works for charities, religious institutions, cultural organizations, governmental agencies, and volunteer organizations. The business strategy is the process that resolves the structural tension between the organization's purpose, and the current expression of that purpose:

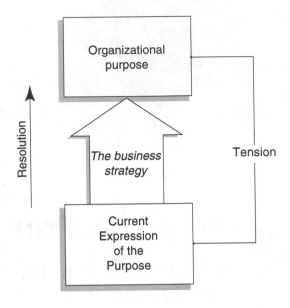

The business strategy answers the question, How does the organization generate wealth or its own viability? When we think about the business of the organization, we are thinking about how the money works. Why does it come in? What happens to it once it is in? What is exchanged for it?

An Exercise in Business Strategy

In some of our training sessions, we help managers develop their strategic business skills by dividing the participants into two groups and giving each group a business scenario. For example, both groups may be told that they are in the microchip business, but one group will be in the commodities end of the industry, while the other group will be in the designer-boutique microchip market. This is the only information given the two groups. They are allowed twenty minutes to develop a business strategy. "On your mark, get set . . ."

How NOT to Think about Business Strategy

Frequently, the people in each group spend their time talking about management stuff, "We should have everyone feel as if they own their jobs," or "We can use cross-disciplined teams in every area." These comments have very little to do with forming a real business strategy.

Often they create goals that show that they haven't any understanding of how their group's microchip business makes money. Typically, people say things like: "We will increase sales 25 percent next year." "We will dominate our market internationally." "We will increase our profit margin to a 23% return on investment." Extraordinarily, these goals have been created in a vacuum. (Increase compared to what? Return of investment in relationship to what?)

When we ask the participants why they wrote these types of goals, they aren't able to answer. They don't really know. These are good people and good managers, and yet there's a loophole in their knowledge.

Many participants did not think of the business strategy as how the organization generates wealth. Why? In their own companies, they had used the term *business strategy* in a different way. Here's how it goes. The boss comes into the planning meeting and says, "Let's increase last year's performance by 25%." So the group makes up goals that are increases from last year's performance. If sales were 100,000 units last year, then this year the goal would be 125,000 units. If gross revenues were 20 million, the goal would be 24 million. So now comes the term *business strategy* in the context of: "Here are our goals. We need a business strategy to get there."

Goals like these do not reflect an understanding of how the business actually works. It just reminds us of the old joke: "Strategic planning, the way most companies do it, is neither."

While some managers in our microchip exercise were in the habit of forming business goals that were merely an extrapolation of past performance, some of them used popular clichés of the day: "We will develop our core competencies" or "We will have total quality" or "We will be customer focused." As we explored the reasoning behind their thought processes, it became clear that no one could build a business based on their approach. Some of these ideas could build a small fortune, as long as we started with a big fortune!

How TO Think about Business Strategy

What's a good way to think about business strategy? If we are in the microchip business, one important question is this:

What *motivates* the customer to buy our products or services?

Notice the word *motivates*. This is a different idea from the old "What are the customer's needs?" Motivation tells us how our potential customers are thinking and feeling, and what their real reasons are for buying our or other people's wares. Cigarette smokers need to quit smoking for the sake of their health. That tells us what they *need,* but they don't always make decisions based on their needs. They make them based on their *motivation*. They may know they need to quit, but their motivation sends them to the corner store so they can act like the Marlboro Man or Joe Camel.

When we penetrate our potential customers' motivation, we begin to understand the business we are in. If we don't understand our customers' motivation, we are very unlikely to understand our business strategy.

The mistake a lot of companies make is this: They think about their customers from their own point of view, not their customers' point of view. They think about all the reasons their customers *should* want to buy from them. "We have value added" or "We have the most variety" or "We have the capability to deliver any time of day" is what people in companies say.

Customers don't make their buying decisions based on added value, but rather, on value itself. Added value is often a rationale suppliers use to justify their price. How much variety a company has is irrelevant to a customer who wants only one item. An organization's capability to deliver anytime is not the reason most customers buy. They care only if they can get the product or service when *they* want it.

The phrase *customer focus* has a lovely ring to it. However, it doesn't answer the question, What motivates the customer to buy? This question leads us to a different orientation in our understanding of customers. We can put ourselves in the customers' shoes and attempt to understand their concerns and values.

Because they have surveyed customers, defined customers' needs, evaluated the competition, put TQM into the organization, and developed their customer service department, many people think they are totally customer-focused. But too often, in spite of these valuable practices, the customers' true motivation remains obscure. This is why the folks around the company can be surprised when, after so much "customer focus," the customer decides to go elsewhere. Why don't they love us anymore? It's us, not them!

And Now, Back to Microchips

In our microchip exercise, we gave the groups a chance to rethink their scenario. But this time we encouraged them to think about their customer's motivation.

Why would a customer want to buy their product?

The Commodity Microchip Strategy

In the commodities end of the business, customers buy from their suppliers for two reasons. First, the products are available when they want them—on-time, scheduled deliveries so they can meet their production timetables.

Second, the product is inexpensive. To someone motivated to keep the price of the product down, chip quality is not a factor as long as quality is adequate. As long as the chip does everything it needs to do in the product, a higher-priced chip with much higher quality would not be attractive.

Available and inexpensive leads to a "tapestry" of other related decisions: where manufacturing plants should be built, how transport and delivery systems should be organized, how costs and pricing should be determined.

Would we build our manufacturing plants in Rodeo Drive in Beverly Hills? Not even if they let us, because the cost would drive our price up past the point our customers would be willing to pay.

Would we build them in a place where labor costs and the cost of living are high? No. We would look for places where labor is inexpensive and the cost of living is also low. We do need a competent labor force. Would we build off-shore? Perhaps, if the country had the right combination of cost and available competent labor and political stability. Perhaps we would look for other advantages, such as good tax benefits and local investment in our plants.

As we think about our costs, we must also consider transport. Our low cost management could be offset by high transport costs, canceling out our advantages. We want a plant we can use for a very long time, so we would need to study factors that influence its longevity. What is the history of potential sites? What are current trends? What can be reasonably predicted for the future?

What might we not be able to predict? Would what we can't predict put us at undue risk? If so, why should we take the risk? Perhaps we need to find a more suitable location that enjoys similar advantages but has less potential risk involved.

What about availability of our products to our customers? How do we ship? Do we have local warehouses, local distribution? Since there are two major factors involved—price and availability—both must be successfully accommodated.

There are other factors as well, one of which is reputation. But reputation must be based on reality: Can we actually deliver the microchips our customers want, at the right price, at the right time? No matter how good our reputation is, it will deteriorate rapidly if we don't "deliver the goods."

We may also need to update our microchips to meet our customers' need for their future products, so we might have a product development division. On the other hand, we might prefer to arrange licensing agreements with other companies to avoid the overhead, something that would drive our costs up. If we license or buy new microchips when they enter the commodity realm, we can limit our costs and stay competitive.

If we were able to make this offer to our customer, would they be likely to say yes:

> *We can supply you with the microchips you want at the quality you want and the lowest cost, and get them to you when you want them with the least amount of hassle. In addition, when you need the next generation of microchips, we will have them for you at the lowest cost, etc.*

If you were the customer, it would be hard to say no to that offer. Part of our marketing job is to tell the story accurately so potential customers know it is true.

When you are able to make an offer your customers can't refuse, you know you have a good business, or you're on first name terms with The Godfather.

The Designer Microchip Strategy

The strategy for the designer-boutique microchip end of the industry would be quite different. Why do customers buy these chips? Our customers are making new high-tech products themselves. They need to meet product-development schedules, since time to the market is one of the most important factors in determining their success.

They need microchips that meet their specs, perform reliably, and must be delivered on time. Innovation, design, and quality of engineering are acutely important. Since these chips are custom-tailored to be used in specialized products, price sensitivity is less important than unique design. You can charge a small fortune and the customers will be happy to pay it, because they can make a large fortune if you both succeed.

Our customer's buying decision would be based on two major factors: quality of innovation and timeliness. So here's the basis for our business strategy: *Reliable innovation in their time frame.*

If we can pull that off, we have a great offering that it would be hard to say no to.

Once we have this essential insight, we can begin to think about the many other decisions that relate to our business strategy.

One of the demands of the strategy is to have exceptionally talented engineers, technologists, and computer scientists. How do we get them? We would make our company the most attractive in the industry. We would pay the highest salaries. We would locate our facilities in "lifestyle" areas that have an excellent standard of living, very good schools, good weather, and so on. We might also think about locating near a major university such as MIT or Stanford. We might recruit future talent by scouting the high-school science fairs. We would certainly headhunt in the best colleges and universities. By attracting the most talented people to our organization, we develop a capacity for innovation that is exceedingly meaningful to our customers.

To ensure timeliness, we would use the same strategy and apply it to managerial talent. We would want the best technical managers we could get, people who could work with our group of superstar technologists.

How would our potential customers know we could produce the innovation they need, reliably and on time? Our marketing approach would emphasize our track record. We might also use a "worth by association" tactic: Perhaps we would hire several Nobel Prize winners to serve on our advisory board, or even invite them into a special think tank. This would help us tell our story to the world: reliable innovation.

Since the boutique end of the microchip business is not price-sensitive, we need to structure our prices high enough to support our cost structure.

Conflicts of Strategies

Each business strategy generates a host of related decisions. If managers in the organization are not cognizant of the strategy, they can really louse it up by making the wrong decisions. When they make the wrong decision, it will always seem like the right decision. The only thing is, they are making the wrong decision from their experience and limited viewpoint, and they don't know how the parts fit together in the structure. They don't know how their decision will drive structural conflicts and change the path of least resistance so that it eventually moves away from where they want to be.

If they had a greater ability to relate the parts to the whole, they would have made good decisions—ones that support the fundamentals of the business strategy.

Once we come to understand the importance of a true business strategy, and then develop one of our own, the criteria for decisions come into sharp focus. We can make decisions quickly and wisely. We can put them into practice easily, for each decision reinforces other decisions, and our unity of direction builds momentum.

Truth is stranger than fiction. This microchip business scenario comes from the real world. The company in question wanted both a commodities and a designer microchip business. But they attempted to fuse these two different businesses into one.

Why did they fail to see the distinction between the two? Partly it happened because they had built a large plant at an enormous expense. Once they had built it, they wanted to justify their original decision to build the plant. As one decision led to another, the factors that each microchip business strategy required were compromised. This made it harder to compete in either business against companies that had realized the nature of the industry and what motivated the customer.

To make matters worse, the commodities and designer microchip divisions were forced to compete against each other for the same resource base. This was due to a structural conflict that developed between attempts to cut costs on the one hand, and build the business on the other. Leadership lost its direction but attempted to regain control by issuing directives that made no sense from a business point of view: "We want 40 percent of our business to come from designer microchips." Where they came up with the 40 percent remains a mystery to this day.

It is hard to create a good argument in favor of being less effective than we can be. But, as structural conflicts dominate an organization, the direction can seem lost and effectiveness is abandoned.

Organizations need to support their purpose through their business strategy. Not only that, the business strategy must be rethought regularly. Leaders, in particular, need to stay in touch with the strategy as an ongoing factor. The business strategy is the basis of structural tension.

Unless a company understands the fundamentals of its business strategy, it will be unable to design consistent and productive management strategies. And without a business strategy, it will be unable to use structural tension to create an organization that advances. It will create a path that oscillates.

How to Develop a Business Strategy

On the basis of my consulting work, I have developed the following questions to help an organization gain essential insights about its business. When you answer these questions, you will come away with new practical wisdom.

- What is our offering?

- Who are our customers?

- What do they want?

- What do we want?

- Is there a match between their wants and ours?

- How do they know about us?

- How do they obtain our offering?

- What is the current market?

- What is the future market?

- How will our offerings change?

- Where are we going?

What Is Our Offering?

What do we actually offer our customers? One company offered customers various plastic tray products. But, as we further explored the subject with this organization, we found that the plastic trays were used by customers to shrink-wrap their retail products. While continuing to sell the plastic trays to many of its customers, the company had begun to develop a new offering: the entire packaging process as a service. They had developed the capacity to take a customer's product, package it, shrink-wrap it, box it, and drop-ship it. This proved to be a more attractive offering to their customers.

In this example, the organization has the potential to offer its customers more than plastic trays. It can take the burden of packaging and shipping processes off of its customers' shoulders. It can take away some of its customers' overhead and fixed costs. If the company manages its organization strategically, it can do a better job than its customers can and do it for less money. That is an offering many companies would find it hard to turn down. It is a great offering.

Who Are Our Customers?

Often organizations presume to know who their customers are because it seems so self-evident, and often their presumption is correct. However, when designing a business strategy, it is essential to rethink this question.

Sometimes the customer is neither the funder nor the user of the product or service. Managed health care organizations, for example, have users (the patients), funders (the HMOs), and customers (the physicians, hospitals, and also patients). We need to determine who is who in such an industry. Who influences and who makes the buying decisions? This leads to our next question.

What Do They Want?

What motivates our potential customers to make the decisions they make? From their point of view, what is in their best interests? What are their values, and what do they value? What are they looking for, and why? (This key point should not be underestimated, for a major dimension to our business strategy will be based on what motivates the customer.)

What Do We Want?

The sales force has just proudly landed a big contract. Big commissions go to them. Suddenly the new workload strains the company's capacity to a point where it is hard to fulfill regular orders. People debate whether we should have taken the new contract. Even as the debate goes on, the enterprising sales force is drumming up more big contracts. We could be in trouble.

Our activities must be consistent with our real aspirations and strategies. An organization can lose its way when it doesn't know what it wants. It can choose to get involved with projects it doesn't care about, or projects that are good from a short-term perspective but bad from a long-term perspective.

A company should not really be "customer-driven." Instead, it should possess its own sense of direction, identity, purpose, and strategy. Without knowing what we want, we might harm ourselves by trying to be all things to all people. We need to stay in touch with what motivates us.

Is There a Match Between Their Wants and Ours?

Once we know what motivates the customer and what motivates us, the question is, What is the match? When there is a strong match, we have the basis for doing business. We can build relationships with customers based on mutuality, so that transactions are in everyone's best interest. We can build a comprehensive business strategy that works and gathers momentum.

How Do They Know about Us?

It is not enough to have the best product in the industry. We may have the greatest mouse trap in the world, but if no one knows about it, the path to our door will be overgrown with weeds. The market must know we have the best product and that it is in their best interest to buy it.

Market research may be useful, but often it gives us mixed signals. If we are not looking for a match between what we do, what we offer, what the market wants, and what motivates our customers' decisions, we can be misled by market research.

Marketing is its own art and, perhaps, science. However, whatever the methods adopted, the organization must make sure its marketing approach is consistent with its purpose, business strategy, style, values, products, scope, and so on.

In a way, everything that touches the customer is marketing—the way we write letters, answer the phone, serve needs, handle complaints, and anticipate future needs of the customer. If we know our business strategy, we can focus our marketing so there is a consistent message whenever a customer is in contact with us.

Good marketing will accomplish several essential objectives. It will tell our potential customers who we are, what we do, how we do it, and what the match is between us. It will also keep the match between our current customers and ourselves visible, so they will continue to be aware of that match.

How Do They Obtain Our Offering?

Once customers know about our offering and want it, how do they get it? How do we distribute it? It is essential that distribution systems be thought through with care. Delays in delivery can hurt. So can the wrong cost structure; distribution costs must fit into the overall economic strategy, particularly in price-sensitive markets.

What Is the Current Market?

This answer to this question gives us the opportunity to rethink our built-in assumptions. Perhaps our market is wider or narrower than we think.

If either is true, what are the implications to our business strategy? Perhaps the current market can include another entire segment we hadn't considered before. Perhaps we need to target our potential customers with an accurate profile of the best customers we currently have, so we can focus our marketing efforts toward those most likely to buy.

What Is the Future Market?

Markets change. To what degree can we anticipate what the future will be? If we are a strong player in our market, we might be able to drive the future. If we aren't, we might lose our market to smaller competitors who are more visionary and sensitive to the times. Both Wang and Microsoft have been the strongest force in their respective markets. As we all know, Wang once owned the word-processing market, but lost it when it did not stay current. As market leaders, they did not drive the future; so, without intending to, they left that to others.

Microsoft, on the other hand, does drive the future in its market. It does so, not because it always has the best software products, but because it is very clear about what it wants, what the customers want, and what the match is. It understands its offering is not simply products or systems of products that are compatible; it offers ease of use from the customer's point of view and experience. It is very aware of what motivates the customer, so it can easily anticipate future trends and invest in technological development that will be relevant in the future. When it is not driving development, it employs an aggressive acquisition strategy that buys out any potentially serious competitor. It does not take its position for granted. It constantly rethinks its business strategy so it is always current. It has been argued that Microsoft has too much power and too much locus of market control. This may be true, but if you were on the Microsoft team, it would make sense to try to dominate your game, even if it offends others. An organization has the right to support its own cause. Other organizations have a right to support their own causes, and we, as a society, must decide if the playing field is fair, if not even.

How Will Our Offerings Change?

Ten years ago, Kodak's film stocks were engineered very differently than they are today. The new film stocks are easier to use and can be used under a wider set of conditions. Kodak has done a superb job of perfecting the new super-16 format, used widely for television dramas and even feature films. Before the 16-mm format was perfected, most television was shot on the more expensive 35-mm format.

Who drives change, the market or the market leaders? Each industry will have its own answer, but as we build our business strategy we need to anticipate how our offering will change. Change is not just more of the same. It can be an entirely different approach to the customer. Good strategy is not something written in stone and then enforced by rigid rules. It is alive, dynamic.

Where Are We Going?

Often organizations can become so myopic that they can't see beyond their nose, and they have a pretty short nose at that. An organization needs a sense of the future. If we think tomorrow will look like today, we are out of touch with reality. It will not. We need to know where we want to go—what our desired state is—and our current state in relationship to our desired state.

By answering these eleven questions, we can begin to better understand our business. These questions help us focus on:

- What we should do

- How we should do it

- How it will work (viability)

- Where we are going

Everyone who makes decisions within an organization benefits from understanding the overall design of the company. Let's relate this to how the path of least resistance works. If we didn't know how our business worked, it's a pretty safe bet that the organization will self-organize into structural conflicts creating oscillation. If we do understand our business strategy, we can develop structural tension that aims everything in the same direction. The structure creates a path of least resistance that moves toward our goals and will create advancement rather than oscillation.

Royal Ford's Story

Terry Ortynsky is the visionary owner and president of Royal Ford, a Ford dealership in Canada. For more than 10 years, Terry has adopted a structural approach in the dealership. He and his management team created a business strategy that was consistent with their purpose and values, which includes honesty, fairness, and great service—qualities that are often missing in many car dealerships.

When they began to redesign their organization, Terry and his team saw that the organization, as it was structured, didn't support the values and purpose of the company, nor did it have a concrete business strategy. Some salespeople sold cars based on lowest price, some on service; some were manipulative, some were high pressure. Systems seemed fragmented, and some departments had an "us against them" attitude.

Royal Ford's Goals and Business Strategy

As the team members looked at what they wanted, they saw that the current organization was inconsistent with their goals and values.

So the team members thought through the business and defined their business strategy, which became this: Royal Ford would provide the best service possible, sell its cars and trucks at a fair price, and treat people with respect. They created a goal of 60% rate of repeat business. This built in a growth trend, because, if they accomplished their 60% goal, every year they would have 40% new business; and, of that, 60% would repeat throughout the years.

The fundamentals of their business strategy were great service, a very good experience of buying a car and having it serviced, the convenience they could give their customers in paperwork, and the fairness of the deal. They weren't going to always be the lowest price, but they would always be the most reliable and the best dealer.

Actions to Support the Business Strategy

Many changes had to happen to put the business strategy into practice. One of the first steps was to put all of the sales force on salary and get rid of commissions. Terry and his team realized that sales commissions created a conflict of interest for the salespeople: Good service, on the one hand, as opposed to their personal gain, on the other. This was a bold step, because they took it just when there was a recession and the market was off. But it defined to everyone that the business strategy and values of the company came first, and financial performance would have to be a product of that. Salaries for the sales force took the pressure off of the salespeople, because they would get their salary no matter how many cars they sold, and they could put their attention on serving the customer by making sure each person ended up with the right vehicle and deal.

Another change that Terry and his team made was to divide the service department into two: maintenance and repair. Maintenance was redesigned so that customers could get the fastest turnaround when they got their regularly scheduled maintenance work done. As the group members telescoped through their structural tension charts, they noticed that the way parts were being distributed to the people in service slowed down the time to do the maintenance. The parts department was in total control of inventory and didn't want the service technicians messing with it. But the team worked out a plan that protected the integrity of inventory and yet speeded up parts distribution; that was to put the maintenance parts right in the shop.

The team members worked with service and set up a goal of 100% first-time repairs, with no needed returns to repair the same problem. They created systems to make sure that the service technicians got the repair right in the first visit.

Another thing they did was to tear down the walls between parts, service, and sales, because they saw that people were isolated from each other, which seems to contribute to fragmentation of departments rather than the whole company working together. When the walls come down and the space opened up, the people began to work more as a whole organization.

The team worked out many other systems to deliver superb service to the customers, and the organization learned, innovated, invented, and experimented. Business got better. Growth led to more growth, and because it was planned growth, the team could plan their growth of capacity directly to the workload.

Ads That Tell the Story

One day I was working with Terry and his team, and I asked them to put their newspaper ads around the room. Like visiting a gallery, we went around viewing the ads. Many of the ads read, "We've got too much inventory! Everything has to go, so come in and get the best price!" Or "Sale, sale, sale!"

The ads told the story of a very different business strategy than the one Royal Ford had. It thus contradicted its business strategy by focusing on lowest price rather than service, convenience, fairness, and respect. "Who wrote these ads?" I asked the team. "Oh, the ad agency writes them." Everyone saw that they contradicted the business strategy. For the next hour, the team went through an exercise I often use with clients. I make them write ad copy, because that is one of the quickest and best tests of how fluent they are in their business strategy.

Soon the room was papered with their new copy. Some of it was awkward, and some of it was rather good. The one that captured their business strategy the most was this simple statement: At Royal Ford, we make it easy.

That is their story in a nutshell. They work hard to make it easy for the customer. They make it easy to buy a car, service the car, arrange the financing, get transportation while the car is in the shop, get reminded of the cars' maintenance schedule, and so on. Now, in every ad and television commercial, Royal Ford's business strategy is front and center. All of the "lowest price" come-ons the ad agency used to write for them are gone. The team often writes its own ads or works closely with the ad agency to make sure its business strategy is being expressed clearly, so the match between its offering and the customer's motivation is communicated well.

Royal Ford is a model company for the structural approach, and its story shows how, within an advancing organization, the path of least resistance is the foundation for more success. The company almost always reaches or exceeds its goals: for example, it consistently accomplishes its 60% return business goal.

Quick Review

What Is a Business Strategy?

- The business strategy expresses the purpose of the organization and defines how wealth is generated. It leads to a tapestry of related decisions.

- The management strategy puts the business strategy into practice by defining how work gets done through the coordination of people, systems, and other resources.

- Managers too often do not understand the company's business strategy and, therefore, make decisions that ultimately conflict with it.

- Shotgun approaches to business strategies cost too much and leave the organization unfocused and undisciplined.

Creating a Business Strategy

- The good way to develop insights that can be used in your business strategy is to answer these questions:

  —What is our offering?

  —Who are our customers?

  —What do they want?

  —What do we want?

  —Is there a match between ours and their wants?

  —How do they know about us?

  —How do they obtain our offering?

  —What is the current market?

  —What is the future market?

  —How will our offerings change?

  —Where are we going?

CHAPTER
12

Frames

The Best Way to See Reality

There are many built-in impediments to seeing reality objectively—
and we must see it objectively to establish structural tension. But the
impediment that stands above all the rest is the usual way we think.

We have not been taught to think. Instead, we have been taught to
use information as a "database" and then compare reality against what
we already know.

This chapter looks at how we frame our thinking.

Framing Reality

When people use Structural Tension Charting, one of the important
challenges is that they must think differently. The change is from
thinking linearly in small units to thinking dimensionally in larger
units.

How do we look at reality? Imagine we had a video camera. We
could shoot a closeup, a medium shot, or a long shot. When we play
the video on a television monitor, the size of the picture would be the
same: 13 inches, or 17, or 21, or whatever the monitor's size; whatever
type of shot we made, it would fill the entire screen. Each type of shot
is a particular frame of reference.

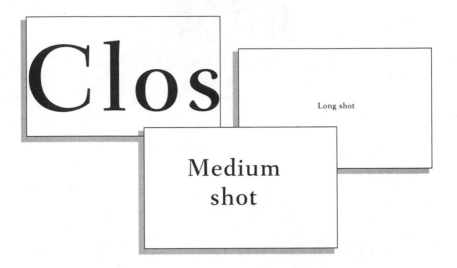

Each of us habitually looks at the world through a lens that is focused on a closeup or a medium shot or a long shot. We can move from one type of shot to another, but usually we don't.

To redesign our organizations, to have the path of least resistance move us to real and lasting success, we need to become very good at seeing current reality. We may need to learn how to observe, process information, and make critical distinctions in new ways. We need to be able to change our frame of reference as easily as a cameraperson can change from a closeup to a medium shot. Let's explore each of these three frames of reference and how to change from one to another.

The Closeup: Immediate Events and Obsessive Detail

Just as it sounds, the closeup frame of reference is so close that you might not know what you're looking at. The closeup shot is focused on immediate events and obsessive detail. Some people use the closeup as their primary frame of reference, focusing on the immediate events that confront them to the exclusion of anything else. They tend to obsess about details, but they can often miss what the various details mean.

Organizations are filled with people who use immediate events and obsessive detail as their frame of reference. We can see this trait by how they relate to time. Time, to these people, comes in short phases. If a conversation is going on about the budget over the next three years or about a product development strategy for a ten-year period, these people will talk about the company's immediate problems. They might pick out a detail from the general overview and focus their attention on it. They think they are adding a missing piece; the devil is in the details, and they are playing a form of devil's advocate.

When managers who are assigned the overall leadership of a project, department, or division think in this closeup frame of reference, they can easily be overwhelmed. It's because of the way they take in information, bit by bit. It is hard to hold on to so high a volume of bits, and eventually they run out of the mental capacity to keep it up.

Such people would see the world as complicated and hard to manage. They might have high aspirations and deeply held values, but their way of relating to information greatly limits their effectiveness. In spite of their aspirations, they would be forced to react or respond to the immediate circumstances in which they find themselves. The experience would be that of treading water.

However, even if you have had your lens zoomed in on a closeup your whole life, you can zoom back. You can change your frame. We have had several people in our organization focused on the closeup view of life. We helped them move back so they could take a broader view. They didn't lose their ability to work with the details, something we valued and needed. But they were able to put the details in context. When they backed up, time passed differently for them. They reported having a feeling of more breath and psychic space.

The Long Shot: Chronic Vagueness

If we back up too far, we can no longer make out what is before us. Some people habitually look at the world through a lens that is so wide that everything seems to fuse together in an indistinguishable haze. They know that something is there, but they can't quite make out what it is. These people think in very long time periods, and they often ponder the distant future more than the current reality.

These days, this frame of reference is more prevalent within organizations than we might imagine, and it takes the form of chronic vagueness. Phrases such as *customer-focused, increased sales, quality,* or *organizational learning* can give the impression that something important is being said. But just what? When something remains that vague, it seems remote—an abstract idea and not a reality.

People who live in the long shot quite often speculate about how the world is, because, without a clear view of current reality, it gives them a way to get their bearings. Managers who are vague often attempt to be inspirational because, if they are to mobilize the people whom they manage, they cannot rely on a concrete world they have trouble seeing. Instead, such a manager will use the tone of the group to determine progress. If the members fail to respond to the inspirational atmosphere, speeches are given, hands are held, and warm feelings are projected. How about a hug! Chronic vagueness makes it hard for these managers to move forward toward their goals because it's hard for them to see reality.

Even managers who think they use a systems approach in their work sometimes are not thinking systemically at all, but merely presuming some kind of "everything is connected and we are all one" worldview. It's okay, man, everything is cool—whatever.

To truly think systemically, one must see exactly how elements are connected and what types of relationships they form. One must notice the system in fact, rather than simply impose a general systems notion on reality.

Since structural tension is formed by the discrepancy between the organization's goals and current reality, if reality is missing, all the vision in the world will not help, and the organization will slip into structural oscillation. And that's not cool.

If you have a long-shot frame of reference, you can change. Qualities such as love, loyalty, selflessness, and professionalism can be real, but we see these qualities in action.

As in the world of theater and films, character is action. We know Hamlet by virtue of the actions he takes in confronting the conflict of loyalties between supporting his mother's happiness and finding justice for his dead father's ghost. Hamlet's character is seen by his actions, not by what he says about his actions. The same is true in "non-fictional" life. Warm-sounding concepts are meaningless until they are expressed by actions; then they can be easily seen.

Once we express our values in action, we have moved from the haze of vagueness to the clarity of shape; we have changed focus from the long shot to the medium shot.

Not a Winning Combination

Some organizations have both a high concentration of obsessively detailed people who are driven by immediate events and a high number of people who are chronically vague. This is not a winning combination. Within these organizations, we seem to have a choice between extremes. We can sloganeer with the company's "visionaries," or we can plow through tons of information that simply overwhelms us. Conflicts within these organizations seem unaddressable. There is no meeting of the minds, for the two different types are speaking an entirely different language. But, because both of these frames of reference are ineffective, no one group ever dominates. When organizations like this attempt to become a "learning organization," some will use the opportunity to preach their various worldviews, while others will attempt to tutor people in how to deal with the minutiae.

The Medium Shot: Objective Shapes, Trends, and Patterns

The medium shot enables us to see both the forest and the trees. We can make out details, but we can also recognize the relationships formed by these details. As we back away from a closeup or move in from a long shot, we reach a point where we can see shapes and patterns. We can see the shapes just as clearly as we see various objects.

By observing from some degree of distance or separation, we can perceive reality with a perspective that leads to understanding the spatial relationships various objects have with each other.

With a medium-shot frame, time is observed very differently than it is from the other two frames. We can see the present but also see how the present connects with the past and how the present may play itself out in the future.

If a baseball player hit a ball toward center field, and the ball was high in the air and moving out fast, we would be able to predict to some degree where it is likely to land. This is why sports announcers can watch a solidly hit baseball sail out toward the fence and say "Going! Going! Gone!" If they couldn't predict where the ball might land, they would have to say "Don't know, don't know . . . oh, wow, it suddenly went over the wall!"

The values in using a medium-shot frame of reference are that we are able to get more usable information than we could otherwise. Both the closeup and the long shot give us information, but they are like nonrelational databases; the information base cannot connect with various other databases. But the medium shot—the objective vantage point of shape and pattern—is like a relational database in which things do in fact connect.

Of course, seeing patterns and trends provides us with insight about cause and effect and about the consequences of the actions we have taken, are taking, or might take in the future. When we study reality on this level, we can be objective. Were our impressions accurate or inaccurate? Were we able to take action at the best moment because we understood how the patterns would play themselves out over time?

We can see the shapes and patterns that reality forms when we are able to move in at will for a closeup if we need more detail. When we need a broader perspective, we can back up for a long shot. In either case, we are able to take in information and relate it to its proper context. We can delve into relevant details but not obsess about them. We can observe reality from a great panorama but not get lost. We can observe reality objectively.

Thinking Dimensionally

When organizations begin to use the structural approach, one of the important changes that takes form is how the members of the organization relate to time.

Time begins to move dimensionally rather than linearly. People do think in linear time frames; there are due dates and start dates. They are not simply slaves to a ticking clock but understand how events take shape in time. Time does not move in only one dimension. We experience a "counterpoint" of different time zones that occur simultaneously. We meet a friend we haven't seen for years, and suddenly all the intervening years can seem compressed. In the waiting room of our dentist, ten minutes can seem like three hours.

When an organization uses the structural approach, various time frames fit together. Short-term results fit together with long-term results. We are able to see the shapes and patterns of time, events, and various networks of relationships.

The organization learns how to think of time from the broad perspective of the purpose and business strategy and, simultaneously, the shorter levels of the management and local strategies. As we monitor changes in current reality, information can be tracked through one level of structural tension charting and transform itself to fit the next higher level. We can move in when we have to, and back up when we have to. We can have conversations with each other that are in the same language.

Choosing the optimal frame of reference is only one step in seeing reality objectively. We shall explore the next steps in the following chapter.

Quick Review

- A structural approach requires dimensional thinking—thinking in multiple units—rather than the usual linear thinking.

- Thinking can be done from a closeup, medium- or long-shot frame of reference.

- A closeup shot is focused on immediate events and excessive details. People who use this frame of reference are often so filled with concern about details that they can miss what the details mean in relation to each other. They can miss the forest because they are so focused on the trees.

- A long shot is vague and ill-defined. People who use this frame of reference often substitute platitudes for clear observations about reality.

- A medium shot is the preferred frame of reference because objective shapes, trends, and patterns in reality can be best understood; details can be understood in context, and the more meaningful details can be better explored.

- It is possible to change frames as a first step in learning how to think structurally.

CHAPTER
13

Discovering Our True Vision

Vision is greatly misunderstood. It's too bad, because without a vision of what we want, we would have a great deal of trouble creating what we want.

A vision of our goals is one of the two essential elements of structural tension. An organization without vision is left to problem-solve its way into an oscillating pattern. It is good to rethink the true value for an organization of having an authentic vision.

Defining Our Vision

The word *vision* has been trivialized to death. Many people in many organizations have discounted vision because it has come to mean vague "Mom-and-apple-pie" statements that never lead to anything substantial. For too many companies, the advantages of real organizational vision has eluded them.

Authentic vision lives. All artists, filmmakers, record producers, architects, interior designers, and other professional creators use vision in their creative process. For them, vision is not nebulous; it is concrete. Many of them could not effectively produce their work if they did not have a well-defined vision.

Let's see how it works in the most complicated and organization-ally relevant art form—filmmaking.

The scenes of a film are shot out of order, because filmmakers need to shoot all the various scenes that happen at one location before moving on to another location. If films were shot in the order that each scene appeared in the story, it would be a logistical and financial nightmare—going back to the same location and again setting up the lights, props, and so on.

The director must have a strong vision of the whole film in his or her mind so that all the parts will eventually fit in with the whole. There are two elements in particular that the director needs to man-age: the performance of the actors, and the technical requirements of camera placement and movement.

Because a film is shot out of sequence, film actors must learn how to jump into a scene as if they were the character going through life in the sequence of the story. Many great actors are able to switch to the right channel when they are asked to perform their scenes. They have a vision of the story and, particularly, of their role in it. In this way, they can turn in a performance that moves forward in the final prod-uct, even though they are performing the scenes out of order.

The director manages all of the actors so that their performances blend together artistically. The director manages the rhythm of the en-semble, pushes the contrasts in certain places, and renders a more subtle effect in other places. Every element is understood in relation-ship to all the other elements, and the unifying thematic principle is the director's vision of the film.

The other major element that requires a vision of the film is how it is actually shot photographically. The industry standard is to use only one camera. The scene is performed and photographed from many dif-ferent angles, over and over. The actors perform their parts again and again while the camera shoots the scene from a different position each time. The actors must perform each take exactly the same way so that the film can be edited together. If an actor has a cigarette in his mouth when he says "Let's look in the closet for the body," he must still have a cigarette in his mouth (and it must be the same brand, the same length, and on the same side of his mouth) when the camera operator moves in for a closeup. The closeup shot may be made three hours after the first shot.

The look and energy of each cut must match the other cuts, so that they will blend together when the film is edited, an exercise that may occur months later.

There are other technical and artistic factors the director must manage, including several crews. Also the director works with other "senior managers"—namely, the cinematographer, the script writer, and the producer.

Filmmaking is a collaborative activity, and common understanding of the vision allows people to collaborate.

Without a vision of the end product and a keen awareness of current reality, the director could not manage the actors and crew. In filmmaking, vision is not a vague notion made up of fuzzy inspirational feelings and sweet-sounding platitudes. It is a clear understanding of the end result. It is the standard of measurement against which all actions are judged and adjusted. It creates continuity within drastically changing circumstances.

Clarity of vision is rare in the world of organizations but it is common in the world of the arts. What we can learn from the world of the arts is the practical advantages of a real vision used as part of structural tension.

Dynamic Urge: The Starting Point for Defining Vision

As human beings, we have various desires that range from altruistic aspirations to base cravings; from selfless inclinations to survival instincts; from simple appetites to more complex longings for love, accomplishment, and contribution.

Sometimes we want what we want because of the situation we're in. If it weren't for the situation, we wouldn't want it.

But there is another type of desire that doesn't come from the situation we are in, nor does it change when the situation changes. This is our *dynamic urge*. This term describes our intrinsic desires.

Our dynamic urge is wired into us. We don't choose to have it, we just have it. We can't get rid of it either, although sometimes we may drive it underground in ourselves. We cannot add to it, take away from it, or fake it.

The dynamic urge is a genuine phenomenon of the human spirit in which people, no matter what the circumstances, continue to want to create something that matters to them.

We see the expression of the dynamic urge in the entrepreneur who loves to build businesses. We see it when the great world leaders strive to express values higher than political power and position. We see it in the great artist, scientist, doctor, builder, and athlete.

We see in those who have been knocked around, defeated, disappointed, and hurt, and then get themselves off the ground and try again.

We see it in children when they make pictures, in teenagers when they pursue their first driver's license. We see it in adults when they help their kids get their license and then lend them the car for their first solo drive.

Organizations, like people, have a form of dynamic urge. This force exists in the purpose of the organization. It is found in the hope people have for the organization. It is a matter of spirit, drive, and energy that is self-generative.

The organizational dynamic urge cannot be synthetically fabricated. It can't be manufactured by adopting certain behaviors. It cannot be declared into existence. You can't fake it, even if you are a good faker in other things. You can't fake that you don't have it when you have it. When it is thwarted, it doesn't go away; it smolders as an undercurrent of frustration that builds over time.

Many people have very strong dynamic urges that they are not able to express in the organizations they work for, and this is sad, because both lose. The person loses time that would be better spent on being involved with something that mattered to him or her. The organization loses because a person with a strong dynamic urge wants to join in any way possible to help create the organization.

When the organization is filled with people who have strong dynamic urges and it, itself, has a strong dynamic urge, then magic can happen. We still need to set up the right structure so that the path of least resistance advances us toward our goals, but the juice is there, ready to be turned on.

I am a big believer in people being true to their aspirations and values. I am a big believer in the organization being true to itself as well.

The Ways We Frame Our Dynamic Urge

As there are frames of reference for seeing reality, there are frames that locate the dynamic urge. To use our metaphor of camera angles, we have a closeup, a medium shot, and a long shot.

The medium shot offers us the best vantage point from which to observe reality. It is the level of object shapes, trends, and patterns. In a similar way, within the dynamic urge, as we will see, the medium shot is the best shot to use to organize our lives and organizations because it focuses us on our aspirations and values.

Once we look at the frames of the dynamic urge, we will then explore the way they combine with the frames we use to view reality in structural tension. Not all structural tension is equal, and this chapter will show how to best position our dynamic urge with our view of reality to be able to create the most powerful structure that creates the best path of least resistance.

The Closeup Shot: A Focus on Appetites and Survival

The closeup shot would focus the dynamic urge toward the immediate, short-term, and instantaneous. This dynamic urge could be seen in the form of appetites on the one hand, and survival on the other. Both focus us in the present.

Some people have oriented their lives toward their appetites for food, sex, adventure, pleasure, or whatever. The person experiences time as if it were made up of short, unconnected moments. Within that narrow time frame, the focus is on satisfaction of some immediate stimulation. For many of us, the closeup aspect of the dynamic urge rears its ugly head whenever we pass a McDonald's and immediate appetites become more dominant than our long-term health plan of a low-fat, vegetarian diet.

When people become obsessed by appetites, it is very hard for them to consider their overriding aspirations or values. Quite often,

conflicts between their long-term desires and their short-term appetites makes them feel guilty and weak. People who know that their
health is threatened by smoking cigarettes often are convinced they
will quit right after "this one last cigarette." The immediate stimulation of the appetite can be more compelling than the longer-term aspiration of health.

We might think of appetites as a tension that leads to a quick resolution. The desired state is discrepant with the actual state. And the
tension is quickly resolved by indulging in instant gratification.

When we are infants, our desires are instinctive. Food, comfort,
warmth, and security are inherent desires that demand immediate satisfaction. As we mature, our parents don't always fulfill our desires as
quickly as they did at first. We begin to realize that there are delays between the initiation of a desire (cry!) and its fulfillment (food, clean di-
aper, hug). Later, as children, we learn that some of the things we
want can be achieved only if we can wait for gratification. If we save
our money instead of buying candy, we can buy an expensive toy once
we have saved enough. We learn to delay the resolution of tension to
support our more important desires. We learn to create a path of least
resistance that supports our desires.

This learning is important to our process of growing up. We move
from an instinctive tension-resolution system to a self-conceived one.
We can begin to think in broader time frames, and this helps us develop the ability to be more effective at creating what matters to us.

All of us have appetites we would like to satisfy. The question is, do
we want to organize our lives around satisfying appetites, or are there
other desires that we care about more? A dynamic urge based on appetites is not the foundation for an organization. Nor is it a good frame
of reference for the members of the organization, because it requires
true discipline from people over time to accomplish very involved goals.

Survival is another immediate dynamic urge. But, unlike appetites, our focus would shift to survival only if it were in question. If
we were in real danger, threatened by war or disease, our dynamic urge
would focus us on staying alive. While this dynamic urge is stimulated
by the situation, it is not generated by the situation. Therefore, it is not
a situational motivation but a true dynamic urge that is activated when
survival is at question.

There may be times an organization faces questions of its own survival. During these times, we need to take drastic measures to save the company.

During troubled times, people often rise to the occasion and deliver extraordinary performances. Wars that threaten a country's survival mobilize people to work together and perform acts of heroism. But, once the war is over and the threat is over, the people return to their usual lives. Survival serves only survival, but cannot serve the cause of a larger aspiration.

Neither appetites nor survival can be the basis of a vision for the organization.

The Long Shot: A Vague Focus

People who have a long shot of the dynamic urge have vague hopes and longings. These people hope that someday their dreams will come true and give them happiness and satisfaction. Of course, these desires are so hazy that people find it hard to picture what they want, let alone organize their actions around it.

We might think the down-to-earth, hard-nosed, real world of organizations is immune to the long-shot type of vagueness, but unfortunately it runs rampant in many organizations. Mission, purpose, and vision statements are usually vague, and so is the business jargon many people use in their conversations.

Using obscure language is a bad habit. Often these words or phrases originate in some fairly wise concepts, but the concepts have been rendered vacuous by misuse.

When an organization doesn't have clear aspirations, it's got to fall back on vague concepts. Because there is room for interpretation, each group in the company may put its own spin on things, and structural conflicts lead to an oscillating path of least resistance.

People know that there is something wrong, but their attempt at a "paradigm shift" may be just as vague as ever. Poor things, they can't seem to get anywhere.

Substituting one vague concept for another leaves you with a vague concept.

The Medium Shot: A Focus on Aspirations and Values

The medium shot of the dynamic urge is best when it comes to creating. All of us have aspirations. The question is, Do our aspirations matter enough for us to organize our lives or organizations around them—to discipline ourselves, make the hard choices, and learn whatever we need to learn?

For great organizations, the answer is always yes—they are willing to do what it takes.

For lesser organizations, the answer is no, although they might talk about aspiration and values until they are blue in the face.

This is not to say their desires are not real. They are. But they let conflicts get in the way, and their path of least resistance leads to oscillation.

Changing the Frame

We can change the frames of our dynamic urges. We can move the focus from vague longings or impulsive appetites to aspirations and values. When we change our frame of reference this way, we can become clear about what we truly want to create.

Since we want to view our dynamic urges using the medium frame, let's explore further what we mean by aspirations and values.

Our True Aspirations and Values

Organizations that are unclear about their aspirations become reactive. They react to their industry's market, their competitors' strategies, the fads that become popular, the immediate problems that surface, and so on.

We will always be confronted by challenges. The question is this: Are we driven by them, or are we driving our own fate, guided by our highest aspirations and deepest values?

When do we know what our true values and aspirations are—when it's convenient, or when it is inconvenient?

An organization chooses its true values and aspirations de facto by the actions it takes, the decisions it makes, and the long-term plans and strategies by which it lives. An organization's choices are the defining moments of its life.

Obviously, when values and benefits are not mutually exclusive, it is easy to pursue them all. But often in life we have to choose among competing desires. The choice we make defines what we value most.

If we say we value innovation while cutting the research and development budget; if we claim to serve our customer, while pursuing ways to cut down on the quality of our products; if we say we want to be a learning organization, while our senior executives never take a course, read a book, or investigate what the other members of the organization think or know; then we are out of touch with reality, or, even worse, hypocrites. We "know where we're at" by our actions, rather than by our claims.

The history books are filled with tales of great men and women who have chosen their aspirations and values over all other factors, even when it was a hardship to do so. What did these people have in them that enabled them to do what they thought was right? There is so much to learn from these people.

Framing Both Our Vision and Current Reality

Let's put together the dynamic urge and reality frames and study their impact on each other when we create structural tension.

Here, again, is the form of structural tension:

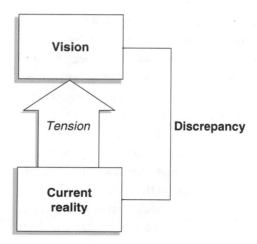

What follows are all nine possible combinations.

Closeup/Closeup

In this combination, the dynamic urge is focused on appetites, and current reality is seen from the perspective of immediate events and/or an obsessive level of detail. Tension leads to quick resolution, as the tendency this structure produces is to pursue ways of gratifying the appetites. If an organization were constituted this way, short-term results and immediate events would dominate the scene. This combination is a difficult one upon which to build a successful company or organization. Unfortunately, we sometimes see this combination when an erratic owner runs a small company. People feel jerked around and everyone exists in a state of chronic frenzy. Success is hard to create.

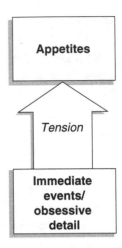

While most organizations are not structured like this, some people are. The closeup/closeup combination does not produce a good manager or leader. Now let's look at the closeup/medium shot.

Closeup/Medium Shot

Appetites, combined with an ability to see broader patterns and tendencies, produce a really odd combination of traits. The person can see the consequences of his or her actions over time, but the drive to gratify appetites seems very compelling. If the person's appetite is unhealthy, he or she would know that indulging in it will lead to terrible consequences because that person can anticipate the overall shape of the outcome. But the path of least resistance will lead the person to indulge anyway. (Do not hang out with this kind of person, unless you are one, yourself.)

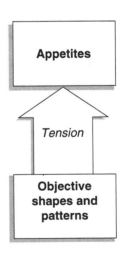

An organization with this structure could see things like market trends, buying patterns of customers, economic trends, and so on. But the organization's short-term demands would clash with a clear view of reality.

Closeup/Long Shot

The closeup/long shot is another combination that does not lead to success. A person or an organization would be in a fog but focused on immediate cravings.

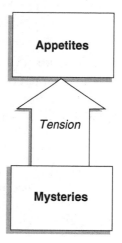

Medium Shot/Long Shot

Here, aspirations and values are the center-piece of the dynamic urge, but it is hard to get a fix on reality. Because it's hard to get where you want to go if unclear about your starting point, the tension formed is very weak and unlikely to become the dominant structure for a person or an organization.

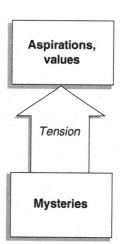

Medium Shot/Closeup

While aspirations and values fill the desired state, reality is so narrowly focused that it is hard to evaluate how effective our actions may be. In organizations that have this combination, people pore over mountains of information, hoping that somewhere hidden in the details is useful information. However, they are unable to see what is really going on because their viewpoint is so myopic.

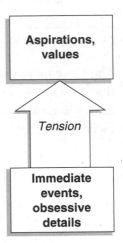

Long Shot/Medium Shot

Objective reality is seen and understood, but the dynamic urge is so vague that the tension within the structure is weak; we know where we are but are not really sure where we want to go. This is a common structure in organizations that substitute platitudes for clarity of vision. Because structural tension is so weak, structural conflicts will eventually dominate the organization.

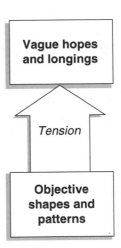

Long Shot/Closeup

The long shot/closeup is not a winning combination. Vague hopes and obsession with details cause the person or organization to long for things to be better than they are, but the demands of immediate events drive a short-term perception. Again, structural conflict will dominate.

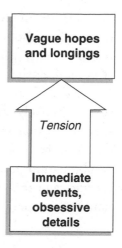

Long Shot/Long Shot

Those with the long shot/long shot combination are lost in space but optimistic. Occasionally we might run into such a person on a park bench, but never in a boardroom.

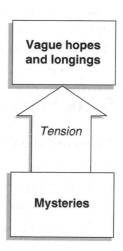

Medium Shot/Medium Shot

For both the individual and the organization, the medium shot of the vision and the current reality is the very best combination for creating structural tension. Aspirations and values form the vision of the desired state, and reality is seen objectively and from a wide enough perspective so that shapes, patterns, and tendencies can be understood. Clarity and caring combine to form a critical degree of structural tension, and this can easily become the dominant force in play.

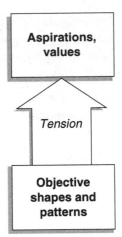

A Final Word about Frames

Here is a final word about frames—the best advice we can give you. Shift to a medium shot in both vision and current reality, and the path of least resistance will support you and your organization.

Quick Review

Vision and the Dynamic Urge

- In addition to current reality, vision is the other element that forms structural tension. An organization that lacks vision cannot create structural tension and will eventually oscillate.

- The dynamic urge is our intrinsic desires; we want what we want independently from the circumstances.

- Like people, organizations have dynamic urges. These are contained in the purpose of the organization, the hope that people have for the organization.

- Organizations view dynamic urges in three basic ways:

  —*A Close Shot*: Desires are seen as goals that must be achieved in the short run.

  —*A Long Shot*: Desires are seen as so distant in the future that they are vague, bordering on hopes and longings.

  —*A Medium Shot*: Desires are seen as aspirations that can be achieved if we discipline and organize ourselves to achieve them.

Aspirations/Values and Advancement

- A medium-shot framing of current reality and vision is the best combination to create strong structural tension. Vision is seen as aspirations and values, and current reality is seen objectively and with the right perspective.

- An organization that is unclear about its aspirations often lets its reactions to prevailing circumstances guide its direction.

- Advancing organizations have clear aspirations and values and take actions that are true to them.

CHAPTER
14

The Power of Shared Structural Tension

A real vision cannot exist when nothing in particular is wanted, no matter how many mental pictures we may form about the future. We cannot have a real vision unless it is based on our real desires. Look to your true desires and you will find the best motivation to act. When people join together who have similar desires, they are able to build synergy—a dynamic in which the combination of the parts bring about some magic power beyond what they add to. Think of the Beatles, the Julliard String Quartet, The Three Stooges, and great sports teams.

What Is a Shared Vision?

Here's a good example of shared vision that can be translated directly into the organization.

In the world of filmmaking, shared vision is common. Everyone who makes critical decisions that affect the final product must have a common understanding of the vision. The set designer, costume designer, cinematographer, actors, composer, sound designers, props person, script writer, and so on—all are making the same film. From the example of filmmaking we can draw real understanding of what it means to have a shared vision.

An organization with a shared vision is a power to be reckoned with, because when the members of the organization share a common understanding of what they are creating and a collective caring and commitment to see the vision become a reality, the first element of organizational structural tension is firmly in place. Shared vision (on a film set or within an organization) is the collective dynamic urge that is the generative juice that powers the enterprise.

Because of the challenges filmmakers must face—changing weather conditions, changing light conditions, planes going overhead—film sets are far from utopian working conditions. But all of the members of the film crew have a strong vision of the film being made. They are committed to its realization both professionally and artistically. Because of their shared vision, everything is tied together. The parts are seen not merely as parts but as pieces of the whole film that must work together.

Without shared vision, filmmaking would be impossible.

Telling the Same Story

Often, there's a basic misunderstanding about shared vision in many management circles. People get confused when they think that those who share the vision must have some say in its creation. So shared vision moves from a vision that people share to a vision that people do not share, unless they have something to do with making it up.

We have to wonder why someone would be less enthusiastic if he or she were not part author of the vision.

In the arts, there is a long tradition of shared vision among professionals—yet the vision wasn't always shaped by the performers personally. The first-chair violinist doesn't complain to the conductor, "Hey, I don't know if I want to play this piece by Beethoven unless I can add a few notes!" The actor does not say to the director, "Look, I think this Shakespeare fellow is a little dated in his language. Let me modernize the lingo, so I can really get my teeth in it."

In 1961, when John F. Kennedy articulated a vision of safely landing a man on the moon, the space program was in its infancy. There was much to do and a whole world of technology to invent. There were principles to discover and challenges to meet. Tens of thousands of people shared in the Apollo vision.

Did they withhold their participation because they did not author the vision in the first place? No, of course not. The members of the Apollo team found many ways to contribute to, and participate in, this vision in which they shared.

When a vision is truly shared, we participate in it because we care about it, and we are glad to support it through our involvement. When we truly care about the vision, it matters little who originated it. What matters is that we see the vision and want to create it.

A playwright was asked how he chose the directors of his plays. His answer was "I have the director tell me the story of my play. If he tells me the story I wrote, we can work together. If he doesn't, we can't, because everyone on stage needs to be telling the same story."

Imagine everyone in an organization telling the same story—by the actions they take and the ways they handle themselves professionally. Imagine that they share a common understanding of the direction the organization is going, and imagine that they truly care about the organization reaching its goals and manifesting its vision. Anytime we dealt with anyone from that organization, we would get a sense of a company that had a shared vision, one that deeply mattered to the people who are part of the company.

From a Shared Vision to Great Values

Shared vision, like great purpose, can be a powerful force within an organization. A vision that best captures the imagination is one that has the ability to move people. The great vision often moves us most.

A great vision engenders great values. And because of that, great participation. This brings us to the ninth law of organizational structure.

The NINTH Law of Organizational Structure

The values that dominate an organization will displace other competing, lesser values.

It is an inescapable law of organizational structure that the values that dominate an organization will displace competing but lesser values. The greater the value, the lower the likelihood that lesser values will be taken into account or be influential.

In light of true greatness, pettiness disappears. When individuals or organizations are pursuing great accomplishments, many of the trivial concerns that might otherwise have been distracting are no longer thought about.

This ninth law of organizational structure cuts two ways, however. If the dominant values of an organization are self-serving, political, and manipulative, then what is trivial will become more important than the accomplishment of a great cause. When pettiness is a dominant value, true greatness disappears.

Greatness can be measured, not simply by size or power, but by scope and character. When confronted by greatness as a dominant value, the organization has something by which to measure and judge every aspect of itself. Is what we are doing consistent with our aspiration and vision? If it is not, we are ready to consider what types of structural changes we need to make. We not only tolerate change, we actively seek it. In light of true greatness, change and restructuring become naturally motivated. As we become clear about the vision we share, we can join together in making change work.

Shared Vision and Choice

When people join together in a common cause, each person makes an individual choice to participate. There is tremendous power in the act of making a choice, for it defines our personal resolve and our intended direction.

When we are forced or manipulated into participation, we rebel. It's our nature to resist autocracy. We may do it subtly through passive-aggressive tricks. We may resist in the privacy of our own mind, imaging poetic justice and good old revenge, or we may do it publicly by causing a showdown and then getting out of Dodge.

However we do it, we resist and rebel. We do it to affirm our own independence of spirit. We do it to save our soul.

You can't have shared vision when someone is trying to manipulate you into compliance, even for the best of reasons. Shared vision implies choice—we choose to join with each other to create this thing that matters to us all.

The Spirit of a Vision Shared

We worship together, see films in theaters together; go to sports events together; see parades together; celebrate birthdays, weddings, and anniversaries together; groove in rock concerts together. We want to be involved with others. And when we are together, a spirit can be evoked that is quite special and sometimes extraordinary.

Sometimes we find this spirit expressed in project teams within a large organization. The team members are able to work together in ways that are reminiscent of the greatest Olympic sports teams. Sometimes we see this spirit expressed in the whole organization itself. The organization takes on a kind of life force that is truly extraordinary—a spirit that moves beyond simply doing a good job to doing something that deeply matters. When that happens, you're glad you're there.

Shared Structural Tension

Shared vision is good, but shared structural tension is brilliant. We share not only in the vision but also in current reality. Together, we hold the tension as we generate our actions.

I want to describe something that often happens that is on the level of the "Truth is stranger than fiction" department. When a team has created shared structural tension, the phone starts to ring with just the person you wanted to talk to. The supplier is able to suddenly get you the stuff you needed. Just the right people apply for the job. Everything starts to work. It can be spooky. I'm sorry to talk about this in a business book that is read by hard-core professional managers, because what I'm describing can sound pretty flaky and new-agey. But this experience that suddenly the universe is on your side is so real that it would be irresponsible to not point it out. The people who have had this experience know what I mean. If you haven't had this experience, you have something to look forward to. It doesn't always happen once a team creates shared structural tension, but it happens so much that we need to find the right words that say, "Sometimes the path of least resistance helps us create what we want to create."

There is a side of shared structural tension that is also wonderful and helpful but less strange and more ordinary. As team members begin to focus together on their goals and current reality, they begin to learn as a team or group. They come to know their vision over an extended period of time so that it begins to develop in them. They witness reality changing, and they know they are instrumental in making it change. They not only learn from their successes and failures, but they begin to have an instinct about how to learn, adjust, invent. They begin to learn how to deepen their ability to work together. They begin to have real intuition about their underlying structures, and they can redesign them to support their collective goals. The path of least resistance leads them to the fulfillment of their vision, and they advance. And what could be better?

Bill Brandt, Chairman of American Woodmark Corporation, a leading manufacturer of kitchen cabinets, related the following story about shared structural tension:

> Several years ago we embarked on a radically different long term strategy which included a five-fold expansion of our product offering from about 20 styles to 100 within six years. Over the prior ten years our offering had expanded by only one or two lines per year, so the anticipated change was huge. At the time the company was experiencing record sales and earnings. Our sales and marketing organization supported this strategy, because they saw the new lines as a way to eliminate critical conflicts among key customers, who had expanded into each others' territories, selling the same product under the same brand. Our manufacturing people, however, feared that such a rapid expansion of the product offering would "blow up the company"; and, given our financial success, they discounted the marketing rationale for this direction. Essentially, the two groups saw both the vision and the current reality quite differently. We initiated the plan by more than doubling our offering to about 45 lines by the end of the second year. While our sales and marketing people were enthusiastic over this period, the general atmosphere within our manufacturing group was one of grudging compliance, with a conviction that any slowing of the transition would help "save the company."
>
> By the beginning of the third year, however, the nation was in a recession, we were losing money, and our factories were ex-

periencing significant downtime. Then early in that year our two largest customers separately informed us that they would be reducing their purchases by as much as 50%—primarily because of the brand conflict. Suddenly, everyone shared the same reality—we were in a crisis that threatened the viability of the company. We made the commitment to do whatever it took to get back in their good graces, including the replacement of existing, product styles which appeared "tired" and "out-of-date" and the addition of exclusive lines or brands if desired. The perspective of our manufacturing organization shifted dramatically from "we're changing too fast" to "tell us what you need, when you need it, and we'll get it done." By the start of the third year, less than nine months from finalizing a revised plan, we more than doubled our product offering to over 100 lines, and we replaced existing cabinet styles which represented 70% of our annual sales.

We had created shared structural tension between a vision of regaining our position as a valued supplier and the reality that our key customers were dumping us. The structural tension generated tremendous energy to accomplish what would have been previously deemed impossible. People throughout the company made personal choices to "do whatever it took," and in many instances it took a lot. During this period we were fortunate that many things did seem to just fall into place to help us along. The new product offering was a great success. It did not blow up the company, but rather was instrumental not only in our recapturing, but also in surpassing our prior position with these customers. Furthermore, completing this task helped create a spirit that we can indeed accomplish whatever it is that we set our minds to, a spirit which has carried forward to this day. The original vision of quintupling the product offering within six years was accomplished in three.

Quick Review

A Shared Vision

- When people have a shared vision—a shared dynamic urge—they can create great synergy.

- Shared vision is the prime generative force that powers a successful organization.

- People can participate in a shared vision and work to achieve it, even though they all did not participate in creating the vision.

- A great vision engenders great values.

- The ninth law of organizational structure is: The values that dominate an organization will displace other competing, lesser values.

A Shared Structural Tension

- Shared structural tension occurs when people share not only the vision but also the current reality of the organization.

- Shared structural tension is a more powerful generative force than a shared vision.

Organizational Greatness
Building on Structural Tension

Once the foundation of an organization has been structured to advance, what can we build upon it? What might we hope for in our organizations? If an organization could be anything at all, how high would we reach? Perhaps organizational greatness.

Great Values Equal a Great Organization

As there are great causes, great books, great medical teams, great music, great orchestras, great films, great ball teams, and great buildings, there are also great organizations. We know a great organization in the same way we know a great sports team: by the way the individual performers work together, play the game, and consistently achieve their goals. We know great teams by the spirit they express, the level of aspirations they have, and the values they live by. We know them by the ways they enrich our society.

A great organization continually takes a stand for its values and dreams. So it must have real values and real dreams.

In this day of acquisitions, some companies are left in a funk. They are owned by a large holding company that bought them as an investment. Their job is to produce profit for the parent company. The parent doesn't understand the business of the company, nor is it interested. The parent only wants to milk the subsidiary for all it can, and then, when the subsidiary has been run into the ground by lack of investment in its capacity or future, it's sold.

The people who work in these acquired organizations suffer from a complex conflict of wanting to do the right thing, work hard, and support the cause, and yet they are treated with indifference and disrespect. What is disrespected is their humanity. "You are dispensable, and you better know it" could be written on plaques on the wall, for it certainly is etched in everyone's mind. People who, before the acquisition, were involved, who cared, who stayed late anytime it was needed, are forced to lose interest, give up caring, and leave just as the clock strikes five.

During a flight from Houston to Hartford, a fellow passenger asked me, "Can an older company change and become new again?" He was working for an acquired company that was owned by some $3 billion company in the UK. As we talked, it was clear that he hungered for involvement, but the rug was cut out from under his company over and over.

Older companies can change and be reborn and can even become great or become great again. But what's to motivate the change? Shareholders' return on investment has never been a big turn-on for anyone, unless you're one of the major shareholders.

The great organizations know that there's more to life than shareholders' return, even while they manage that part of their business. Great organizations are not just organizations that spout a bunch of platitudes every morning before the workday begins. They walk more than their talk, and they are able to be true to themselves. They also tend to make a lot of money. Isn't that wonderful? Greatness often is a commercially viable proposition that pays off handsomely.

What kind of organization would you rather work for? One in which you could express what is highest in your spirit, or one that doesn't care about you personally but just needs someone like you to do a job so it can make more shareholder profit? Where would you work? Not too many people would choose the latter organization. What does that tell us about ourselves? That we would rather be a member of a company that stands for values, that reaches for its future, that cares about its people than one that doesn't.

Some organizations seem to evoke in us a call to be our best and most noble.

Great organizations are, in microcosm, what great civilizations are in macrocosm. They have a strength that goes beyond any individual, but this strength is dependent on the involvement of many individuals.

The leadership in these organizations is great, wise, and dynamic, but the great organization can outlive its leaders, while the lesser organization cannot. Why?

The Elements of a Great Organization

Above, we described what a great organization looks like, but let's now be more specific and discuss the elements of organizational greatness, elements that you can use in redesigning your organization. These elements are as follows:

- Power is distributed widely and well.

- Local relationships are soundly managed with overall interests in mind.

- The organization itself is a social force.

- Principles determine policies.

- Expansion is clearly defined.

- Resources are managed in ways consistent with the comprehensive design.

- The organization continually aligns people.

Widely Distributed Power

Alexander the Great was history's first world leader. During his life, he unified the ancient world, first through conquest and then through forming fair and equitable local governments. But, because he was not able to distribute power widely and well, his world fell apart when he died.

Like Alexander, there are great organizational leaders who do not distribute power widely and well. Therefore, while they are able to bring their organizations to a level of greatness while they reign, the organization fades as soon as they are gone.

We all have been schooled in the fall of Rome: how it became complacent, self-indulgent, and self-destructive. But there is much to learn from the opposite end of the story, the rise of Rome. Before the age of Caesars, Rome grew out of the cooperation of farmers who were able to join together in a true commonwealth. They created stability by the wide distribution of power that was held in their senate, one of the first governing bodies in history. They hadn't had any leaders that were as brilliant as Alexander, but as farmers, they understood how nature grows and changes, and they built a civilization that lasted a thousand years. When power became centralized, and was no longer widely distributed, their days become numbered.

Soundly Managed Relationships

Structure is formed by relationships. As we have seen, many structural relationships in organizations are formed inadvertently rather than by design. Building a path of least resistance to greatness includes the ability, wisdom, and inclination to manage the relationships of the essential parts of the organization. Managing the parts does not mean to micromanage them or manipulate them. It means to understand them and help tie them together. This has to be done from the top for the organization to reach greatness. But it also has to be done from the various positions that people play. It is so easy to think about our concerns and ignore the system of relationships we are in. It is so easy to think of "us" and "them" and ignore how we, together, form the structure.

Rome knew how to bring the parts together when it was on the ascent. Once it lost that knowledge, it had to fall, because it could no longer make decisions in its enlightened self-interest. It could only make decisions in its self-interest. The former is truly win-win; the latter is win-lose in which everyone loses in the end.

To manage the organization's relationships, one needs to have a different orientation than we usually see in most organizations. But then again, greatness is uncommon and special. For those of us who aspire to organizational greatness, we welcome such a change of orientation if it is needed.

The Organization as a Social Force

CNN is seen worldwide and has brought the whole world together during times of triumph or peril. Microsoft has become a social force, influencing the ways people use computers. Today we know more and more about the effects of diet on health, and the availability of health foods has had a great impact on society. Cyberspace is more than a social force; it creates its own society. Great organizations within industries such as airlines, telecommunications, or high technology are social (even civilizing) forces. Their opportunities to build a world that can advance is unending. Great organizations are active members of their civilization.

Often this is a by-product of the work they do. However, there is also a high degree of social awareness and the ambition to contribute and help build something better.

Sometimes this principle manifests itself in the participation of the organization with the communities where it resides; it can help the economy, enhance quality of life, better the schools, and develop better health care systems while contributing to cultural enrichment through support of the arts. Other times, the ideas and inventions of great organizations dramatically change people's lives for the better.

It is hard to think of a great organization that didn't have a social impact and an interest in having social impact. It certainly begins with the leaders, but it continues with the members. These are people who know that the world they live in is larger than their business.

Principled Policies

In great organizations, policies are determined by consistent principles and values. It would be impossible for an organization to sustain its greatness for long if its policies were inconsistent or unfair or if policies were improvised by the whim of egocentric managers. Like the rule of law, rather than the prerogative of dictators and kings, when principles determine policies, continuity and fairness contribute to organizational greatness.

And the values and principles must continually be rethought. If they aren't, the policies will have an artificial and hollow ring to them because, while they were once the expression of a vital force, they no longer understand their source. Rethinking principles sometimes leads us to change our minds. If that's the case, we need to reexamine our polices to see if they are still expressions of our principles. And if they no longer serve our principles, we must change them, because our policies must be relevant, if we are to aspire to organizational greatness.

Clearly Defined Expansion

Indiscriminate growth and expansion reveals lack of direction, purpose, and strategy. Great organizations understand that growth is neither a good nor a bad thing in and of itself, and so growth and expansion are always well motivated strategically.

In great organizations, expansion always reinforces the purpose of the organization. It is never arbitrary, mindless, or disconnected from the true purpose of the company.

Resource Management Consistent with Overall Design

In this age of cost-cutting and downsizing, a mindless feeding frenzy of reducing expenditures has led to some of the most destructive and silly behavior we have ever seen. If the behavior didn't tear peoples' lives apart, it would seem like a Dilbert cartoon on steroids. What we know from our understanding of structural conflicts between growth and capacity is this: Growth and capacity are inextricably tied to each other. If your organization has growth goals but doesn't have capacity planning that is calculated to support the growth, your organization is simply not thinking structurally or systemically and will oscillate.

It is a practical idea that higher volume (of sales, output, service, manufactured items, etc.) must be supported by adequate capacity. If you add capacity when you need it, you have waited too long. If you add capacity too soon or too late, it will cost you too much.

In great organizations, resources are managed carefully, because that care creates organizational discipline and an economy of means. Managing resources carefully includes the human resources.

All great civilizations managed their resources well, which allowed them to build cities, roads, buildings, and institutions, as well as to defend themselves against their enemies. They invested in their growth wisely, with design and purpose.

These great civilizations declined when they no longer had a vision in which to invest. They began squandering their resources, going through periods of waste followed by periods of cost-cutting that eventually dissolved the fabric of their civilization.

A parallel cycle is occurring every day in many of our best organizations. While study after study has proven the absurdity of many downsizing and excessive cost-cutting practices, senior managers seem to be numb to the business consequences they are causing themselves and the human consequences they are causing their people.

We see the organization's resources in its intellectual capital, facilities, people, ideas, spirit, financial capital, and many other factors that cannot simply be listed by the accountants but that contribute to the asset base of the company. A great organization understands and respects the relationship of its resources to its real work and never mindlessly dismantles its resources base. Instead, the resources are used to create the organization's goals.

Continuing Alignment of People

In Asia, many organizations begin the day with rituals designed to establish and reinforce the spirit and identity of the company. In the West, we have morning meetings, newsletters, E-mail, video presentations, and other types of communications that are designed to align the people who are part of the organization. Means of communications are only as good as what is communicated if it is to lead to real alignment. After all, what gets aligned? Our goals, our aspirations, our values, our social norms, our experience working together, our hope for the future, and our human spirit.

Alignment can happen spontaneously, but great organizations create systems that continually align people with their true caring about what the organization is trying to accomplish and how that connects to the members. Alignment is never assumed, it is managed.

What is necessary to create alignment?

• People share the same values.

- People want to work together toward common outcomes.

- People consciously choose to belong to the organization.

- People are motivated by a deep desire to contribute to the organization.

- The organization presents "a fair game," one in which people can succeed or fail based on the merits of their actions rather than on political intrigue.

When these factors are present, alignment is more possible, but even then, is not guaranteed. The great organizations rekindle alignment by establishing formal methods dedicated to that purpose. It may not be morning rituals in the Asian style, but it serves the same function.

After they mature, organizations often become stodgy and complacent, attempting merely to maintain what they have. Organizations fail when they lose interest in their own aspiration and purpose. Then people have no reason to align.

The great companies stay in touch with the most generative characteristics of the human spirit—invention, exploration, creation, and purpose. Alignment comes from the reality of these qualities.

A Structure: Foundation for Greatness

Many of the men and women who built the great organizations understood the inescapable laws of organizational structure instinctively and intuitively, but sometimes they were not able to institutionalize them and bring their understanding to a new generation of managers. They weren't able to pass on what they knew.

Some organizational leaders are able to pass the principles of structure on, and so it continues and grows.

Can a design in which the path of least resistance leads to advancement be passed on? Not usually. But what can be given to the organization's future leaders is the knowledge of how to create and build and of what structures are best suited to creating and building. If we inherit only forms but not understanding, we won't know why these forms work, and we will eventually change them, perhaps into a structure that oscillates.

We are organizational, structural designers as well as managers. We are able to see beyond the situation and imagine a future we want to help create. And the road to move from here to there is the path of least resistance formed by an underlying structure that supports our hopes.

Quick Review

- Organizational greatness is not a utopian ideal; rather it is found in how an organization takes a stand for its aspirations and values.

- Many great organizational leaders understood the inescapable laws of organizational structure intuitively and instinctually. Unconscious competence limits the ability to expand this understanding throughout the organization.

- To achieve organizational greatness, the following elements must be in place:

   —Power is distributed widely and well.

   —Local interests are managed with overall interests in mind.

   —The organization becomes a social force.

   —Principles determine policies.

   —Expansion is clearly defined.

   —Resources are managed within a comprehensive design.

   —People are continually aligned systematically.

- Structure is always there for us to see. When people begin to understand and use structure to help them design their organizations, true greatness becomes possible.

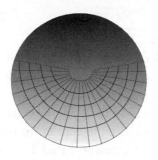

Epilogue

When organizations understand the laws and principles of structure and how these create their paths of least resistances, they can rethink, reinvent, and redesign themselves. They can reach new heights of accomplishment and greatness that had not been within their reach in the past. From our knowledge of structure and how it works, we can begin anew.

Structure is always there for us to see. It is not a model we need to impose on reality, nor is it a belief system we need to develop. It is not a matter of blind faith or metaphor. It is a matter of learning how to see what is truly there—the forces in play, the interconnectedness of parts to wholes, the network of relationships that form patterns of behavior.

This type of insight can lead us to wisdom.

It is uncommon for people within organizations to think structurally. This is a situation this book seeks to change, for without a structural understanding, people will make the same mistakes they have always made. They will do their best, but if the structure does not support them, their best efforts will not succeed. When people begin to understand the vast power and beauty of structure, they will no longer be trapped by innocent ignorance. Rather, they will be able to work with the natural forces in play and create a path of least resistance that leads them to reach for what is highest in them.

Structure is all around us in the natural world. It is dominant in the arts, as well—in every film we see or song we hear. It is in every television commercial we view, and in every rock video on MTV. It is the basis for so much of our world that it is astonishing that it has been so invisible for so long within our organizations. To see it, know it, begin to understand its impact, become able to predict the behavioral patterns it generates, and finally master it so that it can be the basis by which we design our organizations, opens a whole world to us that is rich with possibilities and hope.

The study of structure does not lead us to conclude that the world is merely an indifferent machine and that our response must be rigid and artificial, unimaginative and sterile. Quite the contrary. The more we study structure, the more we are able to appreciate its splendor and strength, the more we are able to work with it rather than against it, the more we are able to understand that, even within our organizations, Mother Nature is at work.

Understanding structure frees us, not only to imagine new possibilities, but also to bring what we envision into reality. It helps us build upon our past, learn from experiences, and also learn from the future—once we master the principles of structural cause and effect and can study the probable outcomes as we find out where the path of least resistance leads.

My hope is this: that individuals and organizations are enriched by knowledge about structure, not only in the tremendously practical realm of performance, but also aesthetically. As the twentieth-century composer Karlheinz Stockhausen has written, "We need to close our eyes for a while and listen. There is always something unheard of in the air."

Knowledge of structural dynamics enables our imagination and aspirations, our values and our hopes, and the depth of our dynamic urge to be the guiding light to the future—to bring about something that heretofore has been "unheard of."

APPENDIX

Some Afterthoughts and Add-on Points

The Notion of Self-organizing Management Systems

With so much interest these days in self-organizing management systems, can structural tension be established and supported by such a system? This is a crucial question for companies that are exploring the premise of chaos theory, complexity, and self-organization.

Because it takes great diligence to create structural tension as the prime force within an organization, we can predict that self-organizing management systems most often will not work. Instead, they will tend to produce oscillating behavior as local forces gain strength and power, only to clash with other local forces.

Chaos, Complexity, and Order

We sit in the concert hall, awaiting the arrival of the conductor. The musicians wander on stage and take their seats. Eventually, there are more than one hundred players warming up their instruments and fingers, tuning, practicing especially difficult passages, adjusting their reeds or strings or mouthpieces or seats or music stands. The hundred individuals perform thousands of acts that are uncoordinated and random. No moment is exactly like another, and individual chance events join with other individual chance events to form a predictable state of cacophony. (Chance events notwithstanding, when it is tuning, every orchestra sounds like every other orchestra.)

An orchestra tuning is a self-organizing system; in other words, it is a complex created by incalculable numbers of occurrences that are self-generated and self-arranged. There is no plan to the multitude of events that occur, but they form predictable and consistent sound patterns.

What can we say about this organization? In many ways, a tuning orchestra fulfills many of the important criteria often described as essential to organizational success:

- It has a common purpose (to tune each instrument to a common pitch).

- Each individual takes personal responsibility for fulfilling that purpose.

- Each member is a highly trained professional, fully capable of performing any task required.

However, this organization—the orchestra—is predictably limited in its ability to produce music within the self-organizing system that tuning produces. When we listen to an orchestra tuning up, we can recognize it for what it is. We do not confuse the tuning with the music about to be performed. If the evening consisted of hours of musicians tuning, we would justifiably want our money back.

But after a short time, the musicians become quiet. The conductor comes to the podium. The baton is raised, and with the first downbeat the musicians produce music that is far more interesting, structurally and emotionally complex, dramatic, and moving than any sounds that came from the orchestra when they were tuning.

We have witnessed a transformation from unharnessed potential that reached a status quo to focused potential fulfilling its promise. What made the difference? Not talent, dedication, skill, professionalism, resources, energy, and attention to detail, for there was no change in these characteristics.

In business, we often hear the call for more of these very qualities. "Our organization needs more dedication, attention to detail, a higher skill level, more professionalism, more resources, more energy." These certainly are useful and important qualities to have in an organization. But, as we can see from our orchestral example, by themselves, these factors are not enough. The composer and the conductor provide vision, leadership and a profound understanding of structure that enables the resources of the orchestra to be put to good use.

The musical score is the most dominant factor. An orchestra with a conductor but without a score would hardly be more productive than the tuning-up exercise. In fact, an orchestra can play a score without a conductor, although usually not as well. So the composer's role is supreme.

But the best score, unperformed, does not reach its height of fulfillment either. The composer, the conductor, and each musician performs a unique function within the music-making process. The separation of function allows each individual to serve the performance of the music. At its best, the orchestra is one of the finest examples of organizational control—the ability of a group of people to join together and accomplish their collective purpose through their shared efforts. Control is multiplied throughout the organization by combining clarity of a unifying principle (score) with competence of personnel (musicians) and leadership skills (conductor).

An organization can be as highly professional as the world's best orchestras once it becomes well-structured, with a thematic unifying principle that is consistently reinforced throughout its various activities. To learn the lesson of the orchestra, we must move away from self-organizing systems that produce limited status-quo results and into a highly composed system that is capable of superior performance.

Structural Dynamics and Systems Thinking: Close Cousins

My friend and colleague Peter Senge has named systems thinking as one of the essential ingredients of the learning organization in his wildly popular book *The Fifth Discipline*. Systems thinking and structural dynamics are two disciplines that are exceedingly compatible, containing many overlapping principles and parallel inclinations. Both encourage people to think in terms of wholes rather than fragmented parts. Both enable people to understand networks of relationships as an intrinsic property of cause and effect. Both enable people to shift their viewpoint from bouts of tunnel vision to a wider understanding of the interconnectedness of events to each other over time. Both encourage organizational learning by enabling people to co-explore the complex issues they face. These are just some of the advantages shared by systems thinking and structural dynamics.

But there are important differences between systems thinking and structural dynamics. Some of them are technical and some are philosophical. It is important to know that systems thinking is not structural dynamics, and structural dynamics is not systems thinking. To better appreciate each discipline, it is best not to attempt to fuse them as if they were different aspects of the same understanding.

Sometimes a systems approach can be better than a structural approach in understanding complexity, for example, when using the tools of causal loop mapping, computer modeling, and diagnostic archetyping. Sometimes a structural approach is better in understanding and describing patterns of cause and effect and trends of organizational performance. Structural dynamics is superior as an organizational design tool for business strategy and management implementation. Since both disciplines exist, we can utilize the best of each.

One of the technical differences between structural dynamics and systems thinking is found in the central mechanism used in each approach. In structural dynamics, it is tension resolution (discussed in the chapter 2). In systems thinking, as expressed in the work on system dynamics by MIT's Jay Forrester and his colleagues, it is the feedback loop.

In its attempt to understand complex systems, system dynamics uses two types of feedback loops. These are called *positive* and *negative feedback*, or *growth* and *balancing loops*. A growth loop reinforces direction; a balancing loop limits direction and is self-regulating.

A growth loop produces the economic principle of increasing returns in which "the more you have, the more you get." Your bank account earns interest, which is added to your capital, which then earns more interest.

While, with a growth loop, more begets more and less begets less, a balance loop regulates and limits growth by comparing a fixed goal with actual variances. The thermostat is set to a fixed goal—the desired temperature. When the temperature in the room falls below that goal, the thermostat turns the furnace on, and it continues to heat the room until the temperature rises above the thermostat setting. At that point, the thermostat turns off the furnace.

Feedback loops combine with other feedback loops to form complex systems. System dynamics use feedback loops as a tool in analyzing and understanding complexity within social, economic, ecological, and organizational systems, and many organizations are beginning to use loop diagrams to explore critical issues they face.

The feedback loop is the basic unit of system dynamics, as words are to language, or numbers are to mathematics. Within structural dynamics tension resolution is the basic unit. A structural consultant will analyze the various tension-resolution systems within an organization that vie for dominance. Then he or she will work with the people in the company to set up new dynamic relationships of tension-resolution systems in which the path of least resistance will tend to move in the direction of the company's goals as a foundation for further fulfilment of the true aspirations and values of the organization.

The Nine Laws of Organizational Structure

THE FIRST LAW OF ORGANIZATIONAL STRUCTURE
Organizations either oscillate or advance.

THE SECOND LAW OF ORGANIZATIONAL STRUCTURE
In organizations that oscillate, success is neutralized.
In organizations that advance, success succeeds.

THE THIRD LAW OF ORGANIZATIONAL STRUCTURE
If the organization's structure remains unchanged,
the organization's behavior will revert to its previous behavior.

THE FOURTH LAW OF ORGANIZATIONAL STRUCTURE
A change of structure leads to a change of the organization's behavior.

THE FIFTH LAW OF ORGANIZATIONAL STRUCTURE
When structural tension dominates an organization,
the organization will advance.

THE SIXTH LAW OF ORGANIZATIONAL STRUCTURE
When structural conflicts dominate an organization,
oscillation will result.

THE SEVENTH LAW OF ORGANIZATIONAL STRUCTURE
An inadequate organizational structure cannot be fixed.
But you can move from an inadequate structure
to a suitable structure.

THE EIGHTH LAW OF ORGANIZATIONAL STRUCTURE
When a senior organizing principle is absent, the organization
will oscillate. When a senior organizing principle is dominant,
the organization will advance.

THE NINTH LAW OF ORGANIZATIONAL STRUCTURE
The values that dominate an organization will displace
other competing, lesser values.

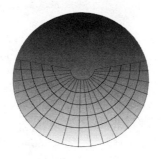

Index

We hope you have enjoyed this book and have found the concepts and principles of value. If you would like information about training in structural thinking, structural consulting services, software and other products offered by Robert Fritz, Inc. you may reach us at:

Robert Fritz, Inc.
P.O. 116
Williamsville, VT 05362-0116
Telephone: (800) 848-9700
                   (802) 348-7176
Fax: (802) 348-7444
E-mail: info@robertfritz.com
Website: www.robertfritz.com

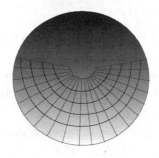

About the Author

Over the past twenty years, Robert Fritz has been developing the field of structural dynamics though his work, first in the area of the creative process, and then in the area of organizational, business, and management issues. He is the founder of *Robert Fritz Incorporated*; *Technologies for Creating®, Inc.*; *The Fritz Consulting Group*; and *RJF Productions.*

Fritz began to lead courses in the creative process as applied to personal effectiveness in the mid-1970s. He began to train others to lead his courses, and more than seventy thousand people have participated in these trainings throughout the world.

His first major discovery was the *macrostructural pattern*, which describes the long-range patterns in people's lives. While each individual's pattern was unique, Fritz observed that there were two general types of patterns that people had in their lives: *oscillating* and *resolving/advancing*. In the late 1970s, he began his work on two basic questions: Why do these patterns exist, and What does it take to change them from oscillating to resolving?

These questions led Fritz to pursue deeper questions about the structural makeup of human motivation. His first major book on the subject was *The Path of Least Resistance*, which quickly became a best-seller. That was followed by his second book, *Creating*. These books, along with the TFC trainings, have introduced revolutionary ideas about the influence of structural causality on human beings, both as individuals and as members of organizations.

In the early 1980s, Fritz began to teach consultants the principles of structure in a course called "The Fundamentals of Structural Consulting (FSC)." During the first few years of its existence, more than two thousand people went through the FSC training. But, the training did not really enable those people to become structural consultants. When Rosalind Hanneman became the London director of TFC–UK, she set out to learn how to master the structural consulting process. She began to transcribe demonstrations of structural consultations that Fritz would do during training sessions and then study them until she could understand why each question was asked and what insight it produced. She continued to practice the fundamental techniques she had learned by using them with her clients, and eventually she began to master structural consulting. Sometime during this period, Fritz and Rosalind Hanneman fell in love, she moved to America, and they married. Rosalind—now Rosalind Fritz—developed the first comprehensive training program in structural consulting, and the first certification in structural consulting was awarded to those who were able to demonstrate professional and technical competence.

As a consultant, Fritz helped many organizations put the structural approach into practice, and his clients include several Fortune 500 companies, many mid-size companies, as well as governmental and nonprofit organizations. Working with other structural consultants, Robert Fritz Incorporated is in the forefront of a revolutionary change in how organizations structure themselves to produce sustained high performance.

Fritz began the study of structure as a composition student at the Boston Conservatory of Music in the 1960s. Later, he studied composition in Germany, and was on the faculty of New England Conservatory of Music and Berklee College. After receiving his BM and MM in composition, Fritz worked as a studio musician in New York and Hollywood, and he won positions in *Playboy* and *Downbeat* magazine readers' polls. Fritz is still an active composer and has written film and television scores, operas, symphonic music, and chamber music. He has written theme music for the PBS business program *Leadertalk* with Garrison Krause. Most recently, Fritz also has been writing and directing films.

Robert and Rosalind Fritz live in Vermont with their thirteen-year-old daughter, Eve.